WOMEN

RELIGIOU

PREMODERN

EUROPE

WOMEN AND THE RELIGIOUS LIFE IN PREMODERN EUROPE

Patricia Ranft

St. Martin's Press
New York

ISBN 0-312-17679-1 paperback

Library of Congress Cataloging-in-Publication Data is available from
the Library of Congress

Design by Acme Art, Inc.

First published in hardcover in the United States of America in 1996
First St. Martin's Griffin edition: January 1998
10 9 8 7 6 5 4 3 2 1

To Michael, Meredith, and Jeff

"For what would become of the world if it were not for religious?"

—Teresa of Ávila,
The Life of Saint Teresa of Ávila by Herself

Contents

Acknowledgments

My interest, respect, and understanding for women religious owes much to the friendship extended to me by the small, pioneering contemplative community at the Monastery of Our Lady of Mt. Thabor in Ortonville, Michigan. Discussions with these women led to my decision to write this history, and I hope it is not a disappointment to them.

I have, of course, incurred many debts along the way as I researched and then wrote this manuscript. First and foremost, I need to thank Annette Davis. Being completely computer-illiterate, I was tempted to abandon the whole project when my editor told me the manuscript must be submitted on disk. Only the fact that I knew Annette would help me out of every fiasco I would get myself into as I learned gave me enough courage to sign on the dotted line. True to my expectations, she was generously there for every silly mistake I made. My student-helper Jennifer Sellers was also indispensable and typed most of the manuscript. Her cheerful willingness to help with any task I asked her to perform was most appreciated.

The Folger Library and the Mullen Library of The Catholic University of America were most gracious in allowing me access to their manuscripts and rare book collections. The Interlibrary Loan services under the direction of Ruth Helwig at Central Michigan University was always efficient and willing to go the extra mile to help. My husband, Michael, read the manuscript as it progressed and made many helpful suggestions along the way. My daughter, Meredith, offered extensive criticism of the text and saved me from many a blunder. I am most appreciative of the time and energy she expended. Friends such as Professor Ulrike Wiethaus, Trudy Bantle, and Beverly Powell offered early and constant encouragement. Karen E. Lenz was most helpful during my European travels. My parents' support has surrounded me during all stages of my work, as has that of my entire family.

The greatest debt of gratitude I owe is, of course, to the three most important people in my life, my husband, Michael, and my children, Meredith and Jeff. Michael's complete and unconditional support for everything I do is the chief reason this work has reached completion. His quiet, ever-present love is one of the greatest treasures of my life. My other two treasures are the best children in the world, Meredith and Jeff. I know this work would not have been possible without their love sustaining me through many a hard time. In so many ways this book belongs to Michael, Meredith, and Jeff.

Preface

Although Anthony (ca. 251-356) is often referred to as the father of Christian monasticism, historians are well aware that he was not the creator of religious life. Athanasius, in his *The Life of St. Anthony,* tells us that before Anthony began his monastic career, he took his sister and "delivered her over to certain chaste nuns who were found at that time." Next he went into the desert to learn by imitating "something about any of the righteous men who were in [that] place"[1] already living the religious life. Prior to Anthony's creation of monasticism, then, women were living the religious life in communities and men were living it in the desert.

Unfortunately we do not know very much about the men and women religious who predate Anthony. Sources are scarce and incomplete. We know that by the third century, ascetics, male and female, were living in Egypt, Syria, Palestine, Caesarea, Spain, Mesopotamia, and Persia. Each group differed slightly from the next, and each emphasized its own particular virtue and distinct behavior. Some lived in deserts and isolated areas, while others lived with families in the middle of cities. Some exhibited forms of antisocial behavior; others were the mainstay of liturgical practices in large urban churches. It was an age of experimentation. Christians everywhere were searching for a more intense way to live the Christian life and forming groups based on a commonly shared practice or vow. The search resulted in what we today call the religious life.

The history of religious life in Christianity is striking in its inspiration and complexity. It has only one constant throughout the centuries, and that is the goal of an intense religious experience of Christianity. Everything else about religious life changes, develops, evolves, or mutates. Numbers, places, types of behavior, practice of virtues, degrees of separation from and involvement in the world, observance of public and private prayer, and services offered to society all vary greatly. Monasticism, with its emphasis on contemplation and separation from the world, was one of the first shapes the religious societies took, and during Christianity's first millennium it was the most dominant form. When we enter the High Middle Ages religious societies become much more diverse. Monasticism remains a significant option, but newer forms that emphasize poverty and the apostolic life—the *vita apostolica*—attract an increasing number of people. By the time we arrive in the modern era, active religious communities are the most popular form of religious societies.

A truly comprehensive history of religious life would fill volumes upon volumes and be the result of a lifetime of research. Perhaps some day such a monumental task will be accomplished. The goal here is much more modest. The present work is a selective history of Christian religious societies for Western women from their origin until the seventeenth century. There are numerous reasons for such a history and for this focus. First of all, there is a pressing need to synthesize the history of Western women's activity in Christian religious societies because it played such a vital role in women's history in general. A proper evaluation of women's position in Western history cannot be attained without knowledge of the history of Christian women religious. While I make no pretense of presenting a definitive history on the subject here, I hope that this work can provide an accessible survey of the major events, places, interpretations, and persons responsible for the various types of religious societies women have formed in the past. Second, progress in the history of women has made this project possible. In the last generation our knowledge of women religious has increased tenfold, thanks largely to scholars working in women's history. In spite of the progress, though, this must remain a selective history, for there are still many areas in need of further research. When computer-assisted projects, such as the pioneering one on medieval women religious directed by Mary McLaughlin, Suzanne Wemple, and Heath Dillard, are completed, we will be better able to offer a more comprehensive history.[2] Third, the history of women religious lags behind that of men religious, and if there ever is to be a definitive history of religious life, this deficit must be eliminated.

Last, in regards to the chronological limits of this study, the history of women religious reaches a natural pause at the end of the seventeenth century, as the whole of Europe enters fully into the modern era. A history of women religious beyond this point would have to include the travels of these women to the Americas and the Far East as they began establishing religious life there. Moreover, with modernity came stronger national identities, and the continuation of the historical narrative would be best reorganized according to this reality. Most important, with the continuing increases in population, urban growth, and industrialization, the sheer number of forms of religious life, individual religious orders, and types of social services Christians engaged in became so great that, again, a historical narrative would need to use an organizational principle different from that used for the period prior to the seventeenth century. All these factors contributed to the decision to end the present study in the seventeenth century. Volume 2 remains to be written.

One of the problems that must be addressed before a history of Christian women religious can commence is the problem of vocabulary. Terms designating those pursuing religious life are often used indiscriminately in ancient and medieval sources and, in some instances, are used quite differently from modern sources. This leads to much confusion for the historian trying to trace the history of these groups. In fourth-century sources, for example, we find reference to women called *ascetics, virgins, widows, deaconesses, ammas, nuns,* and *canonesses.* What we are not told is what distinguishes one from another. At what time or what place, or with which additional characteristic, does the virgin become a nun, or the widow a deaconess? The situation becomes more complicated as we approach medieval sources and is nearly enigmatic in the premodern era. For the modern reader unfamiliar with the jargon of religious life, the situation is even more problematic than for the scholar, for some terms that have a commonplace meaning possess a technical connotation in religious literature. *Religious life, sister, orders,* and *women religious* are examples of such terms. Effort has been made to define ambiguous or unfamiliar terms within the text, but it may be helpful before proceeding further to discuss some of the terms now.

Religious life refers to any and all attempts to live an intense, Christian life distinct from the larger community, and the phrase *women religious* is used here to designate those women pursuing such a life. These are the most broad and inclusive terms discussed. An *ascetic* is one who practices acts of self-denial and mortification in order to be purified and to attain sanctity. Virgins, widows, deaconesses, canonesses, ammas, anchorites, tertiaries, beguines, oblates, *beatas,* sisters, and nuns are also ascetics. All of these groups except tertiaries and *beatas* embrace the virtue of celibacy. Christians singled out celibacy as essential to any who desired to live an intense religious life. In the New Testament and in patristic writings virginity is exalted and envisaged for both men and women, but in second century texts the term *virgin* is restricted increasingly to refer solely to women. A custom developed in late antiquity in which women desiring the life of a virgin were publicly consecrated as such and "received the veil" or "took the habit" (a habit is a designated dress). Not all virgins underwent public consecration though. Many took a private vow and were known only to God. Being a virgin was not a prerequisite for membership in the other groups.

Widows in the context of religious life are women with deceased husbands who vow not to remarry and to remain celibate and who enter a recognized order of widows. The order of widows was the oldest order for women in the church. Different sources attribute different ministries to them: teaching, visiting the sick, praying, and counseling. Mention of them in sources dwindles by the third century, and eventually they are heard of no more.

Also by the third century *deaconesses* as an order began to appear. Deaconesses are mentioned in apostolic times, but in the third century the term is used to imply an office parallel to that of deacon. Deaconesses were found exclusively in the Greek and Syriac churches, and there may have been a separate ordination ceremony for them. They ministered to women in much the same way as the order of widows did.

Canonesses are harder to define. The term appears in the Eastern church late, in the fourth century, and at first was applied to widows and virgins active in the apostolate who lived under certain rules (or canons) of the church. The term was not used in the West until the Early Middle Ages and today is often confused with names for women living the monastic life, especially since the institution of canonesses developed in two directions. One group, called *secular canonesses*, were widows and virgins whose lives were shaped by church rules; the other group, *regular* (from the Latin *regula*, rule) *canonesses*, were widows and virgins who adopted monastic observances. After almost disappearing from the sources in pre-Carolingian times, canonesses returned to historical view in the ninth century and quickly proceeded to enjoy their most prosperous period in the High and Late Middle Ages.

Ammas (desert mothers) are virgins who lived the ascetic life in the desert prior to the spread of institutionalized monasticism. Their lives and practices are virtually indistinguishable from that of the *abbas* (desert fathers). *Anchorites* are women who lived a hermitlike existence outside a set monastic or ecclesiastical rule. This type of life became popular in the High Middle Ages. During this period and in the Late Middle Ages many women were enclosed in structures attached to churches and dependent on the parish for subsistence.

Tertiaries are lay members of a a religious third order. The first order was for clergy, the second order for women, and the third order for the laity. Franciscans and Dominicans were the most popular third orders. Certain women religious called themselves *oblates*, but there does not seem to be any significant distinction implied by the term. Its use in reference to religious orders, however, is entirely distinct from its use in reference to children offered in oblation by their parents to monasteries. *Beatas* were married or single Spanish women who pursued an ascetic, mystical religious life, and *beguines* were women religious who were members of communities that did not follow an approved religious rule. Beguines flourished in the Low Countries during the Late Middle Ages and were free to leave their community at will.

The term *sister* is a common and imprecise term that is applied indiscriminately to any member of most of the groups already mentioned. When we approach the modern era it is sometimes reserved for women who belong to an active religious order, but even this distinction is blurred by the fact that the term sister also is used as a form of address for all women religious. The term *nun* is likewise imprecise. At some points in history it refers to women religious who take public vows. In other periods it designates only formally recognized women religious. Once active orders become accepted, *nun* often is used to distinguish a woman religious in a contemplative order from a *sister* in an active order. Both nun and sister will be employed here as generic, nontechnical terms, synonymous with women religious.

A *foundation* is the establishment of a new religious house. A *religious order* refers to a group of religious houses that are united under one common authority. During the Middle Ages it became customary for religious orders to have their rule approved by the papacy. Such recognition would place them under the protection of church law. Church law is called *canon law*, so the phrase "canonically approved order" often is used to express the full legitimacy of an order. In sixteenth and seventeenth century texts, the terms *institute* and *congregation* sometimes are used in place of *religious order* to avoid some of the limits canon law placed on religious orders, but the reality behind all three terms is nearly the same. A *papal bull* is a formal decree issued by the pope and sealed with a *bulla* (a round seal, usually lead, with a red imprint). The terms *clergy* and *priest* refer to men who are ordained. *Monks* are members of a monastery. The term does not necessarily imply that they are ordained priests, but by the High Middle Ages almost all monks were also priests. Besides referring to church law, the word *canon* can refer to a priest on the staff of a cathedral. In the Middle Ages such a priest is called a *canon secular;* a *canon regular* is a canon who follows a monastic *regula*, rule. The text hopefully illuminates most other terms.

The material is organized chronologically and emphasizes that which is new in each period. Because of the introductory nature of the book, effort has been made to keep academic paraphernalia to a minimum. The select bibliography at the end of the text is meant to supplement the primary sources used in the narrative. It includes only those additional works that I found particularly helpful or insightful in comprehending that chapter's topic and is by no means meant to be exhaustive or even to include the main works on each topic. These bibliographies, plus the primary sources documented in the text, provide the reader with at least a point of departure for further research on most topics. The reader should remember that given the accelerated pace of research into women's history, some of what is written here may need revision in the near future. Where an English language translation of the original text has been unavailable, I have translated the original text.

1

The Beginning

The search for an intense Christian religious life dates back to apostolic times and manifests itself primarily in the practice of asceticism and the adherence to chastity. Women were actively involved in the search from the beginning. During the first two centuries of the Christian era women pursued their goal individually and most continued to live as virgins, whether publicly or privately professed, in their parents' homes or in a similar house setting. Increasingly during the third century virgins chose to live in groups (parthenons), many times still in a family home. Ammon, "chief of the monks who were in Nitria," had a wife who lived thus. After they promised themselves to virginity in their wedding chamber, "he departed to the country of Nitria, and the maiden herself called all the members of her household to virginity, and turned her house into a nunnery."[1] If the structure of virgins' lives became undisciplined, theologians would chastize them, as did Cyprian (ca. 210-258). The church occasionally responded with regulations. Such was the case in Spain: The council of Elvira (ca. 300) addressed the problems created by certain groups of virgins practicing asceticism at home in the Granada area. Other communities responded by placing deaconesses in charge of virgins. Publia, a widow in Antioch, is the first such deaconess known by name. She was in charge of a group of consecrated virgins housed together in her home. Such an arrangement apparently worked, for by the end of the fourth century deaconesses frequently were found in charge of virgins.

Most ascetics were revered as models of holiness for the whole community to imitate, and problems were the exception. This is well attested to in the stories of the ammas, who were loved and honored by all. They were judged on the same basis as were the abbas and had the same opportunity to excel and to influence others. When abba Piterius got too proud of his penances, an angel appeared and put him in his place by telling him about "this woman who is far more excellent than thou art."[2]

There were not as many women in the desert as men, but if they lacked quantity they did not lack quality. Around the year 420 a bishop named Palladius took upon himself "the task of cataloguing the holy fathers in the spiritual life . . . and not only of men famous for their strict way of life but of holy highborn women too"[3] whom he had met during his sojourn in the desert during the last decades of the fourth century. The result was *The Lausiac History*, a text that contains the most complete picture we have of desert life. Its portrait of women is varied and interesting, and it lacks the pervasive misogynism often found in patristic theological writings. Of the 177 individuals Palladius mentions, thirty-five percent of them are women. At one point Palladius tells us 18,900 men and 3,095 women lived in these desert communities. (Elsewhere, Palladius writes that in the city of Oxyrhynchus he found 20,000 virgins living there and 10,000 male ascetics.) Women were clearly quite essential to the movement. Eleven of the 177 individuals in *The Lausiac History* are cast in a bad light; six are men and five are women.[4] When women are discussed as objects of desire, they are passive, arousing lust unwittingly and unintentionally, without guilt. Negative discussions of women are almost absent from the history. Instead, they are portrayed as leaders in the desert experiment. They excel in asceticism, learning, and spiritual discernment. The men display open respect for the women and have no problem submitting themselves to any holier ascetic, be it male or female.

As the third century ended, formal monastic communities emerged. Perhaps women even more than men provided the impetus for two changes that propelled asceticism toward institutionalized monasticism: the triumph of the communal (commonly called cenobitic) life over the solitary (that is, eremitic) life and the harnessing of the ascetic life into a structure with rules and vows. Early on, women realized that both changes were to their advantage. A community and a structure offered women protection, security, freedom, and status in a world where these were often lacking. There are stories of women hermits, but they are scarce in comparison to the stories of women living in community with set rules even while men were still busying themselves with the development of the eremitic life. "Now in the city of Antinoe there were twelve nunneries, and the women thereof conducted themselves according to a rule of beautiful spiritual excellence. . . . And there lived with [amma Talis] sixty virgins who followed the path and rule of the ascetic life in purity, and they led a life of happiness under the teaching of this good woman."[5] Abba Serapion continued his life as a desert solitary among other male solitaries while a woman he converted went to live in a female community with rules.

Traditionally, Pachomius (ca. 292-346) has been designated as the founder of the first full-fledged cenobitic monastery. Recent research reinforces this thesis. With Pachomius and his rule historians start talking about monasticism as an institution. While we have no evidence that women helped in the writing of Pachomius' rule, evidence does indicate that women were involved in the formation of Pachomian monasticism. When Pachomius wrote a rule for himself and his fellow monks, he also wrote one for his sister Mary and her nuns. An enclosed monastery in Tabennesis was built for the men to live in, and another was built for the women. The general impression of the two monasteries is one of compatibility, cooperation, and mutual reliance on one another. They shared the same manual laborers and were buried in the same cemeteries. The monks built the nuns' monastery and the nuns made the monks' clothes. Together they created a monastic spirituality.

THE ROMAN CIRCLE

While Mary and her successors were ruling over their monasteries in the East, other stimulating events were occurring in the West. Women ascetics were increasingly forming groups throughout the Mediterranean, especially in Rome. From these groups came the first forms of independent female monasticism and some of its most revered leaders: Marcella, Lea, Paula, Eustochium, Blesilla, Asella, Melanie the Elder, Melanie the Younger, Albina, Fabiola, Marcellina, Macrina, and Olympias. Too often modern historians have mentioned these women only in association with great male theologians. Their contemporaries were not as distorted in their understanding. These women had reputations and identities in their own right, independent of their male friends and relatives. Basil (329?-379) was recognized as "the Great" in his own lifetime, but his contemporaries also knew that it was his sister Macrina (330-379) who "took him in hand"[6] and converted him to the ascetic life. The scholarship, boldness, and spirituality of Jerome (347-419) were renowned throughout the Mediterranean, but when pilgrims went to Bethlehem they flocked to Jerome's friend Paula, not Jerome, as he was the first to admit: "Who does not allow that what strikes the pilgrims from all parts of the world who come to Bethlehem is Paula herself! . . . Paula, from the very depths of her humility, eclipses us all."[7] All these female monastic leaders were as revered in life as in death, as were their male counterparts, and if they deserved it, as Paula did, above all male monastic leaders.

Marcella

The movement that all these women participated in had its origin in fourth-century Rome. The city was in dire need of moral rejuvenation, and response to the crisis came from an unlikely portion of society, wealthy patrician women. In the home of a widow named Albina, Athanasius (ca. 293-373) and two monks visiting with him from the desert came to tell the story of the austere feats being performed by the monks in Egypt. Albina's young daughter Marcella (325-410/11) was captivated by the tales and kept them alive in her memory. Years later, after a seven-month-long marriage, Marcella found herself a widow and not inclined to marry again. Instead, the tales of asceticism told to her as a child excited her once again, this time to the point of motivating her to attempt her own version of the life. She made her palace on the Aventine Hill into a convent. She followed a routine of prayer, fasting, almsgiving, and corporal works of mercy, but was still not satisfied.

At the age of twenty-seven (ca. 354), she took a step that earned her the distinction of being the first Roman patrician woman to pledge herself to *propositum monachorum* (monasticism): She put on a religious habit (often referred to as receiving the veil). Such an act brought with it ridicule and scorn. "The thing itself was strange and the name was commonly accounted ignominious and degrading," writes Jerome when describing Marcella's action.[8] With Marcella and her public witness the attitude Romans had toward monasticism began to change. Marcella was not a grubby, impoverished street wanderer like the ascetics Romans often saw. She was a powerful, intelligent matron from an illustrious ruling family who was being sought after in marriage at the time of her decision by one of the empire's most eminent leaders, consul and senator Cerealis.

The notoriety placed Marcella in the spotlight, and her behavior and virtue held up well under this scrutiny. Others eventually joined her. Her mother, Albina, began to share Marcella's ascetic practices quite soon after she had begun them. Albina was followed many years later by Sophroni and Felecita, about whom only their names are known, and by Marcellina, daughter of the prefect of Gaul and sister of Ambrose (339-397). She received the veil personally from Pope Liberius on January 6, 353. While her mother was still alive Marcellina lived as a consecrated virgin at home, but upon her mother's death she joined Marcella's group in the Aventine palace, lending even more prestige to the group. As the group's prominence grew, others imitated its example. Lea, occupant of perhaps the highest position in Roman society, shocked everyone when she quite suddenly set up a community in her home. While Lea and her community were distinct from Marcella's, they became associated with the Aventine palace, as did the patricians Asella, "glorious pattern of chastity and virginity," and Fabiola, whose spectacular public penance and subsequent embrace of the virginal life captured Rome's imagination.[9]

Marcella spent the rest of her years in Rome, watching women's communities increase and flourish, and reigning as scripture expert. Jerome, the most distinguished scripture scholar of his era, tells us that "after my departure from Rome, if any argument arose concerning the testimony of the Scriptures it was to her verdict that appeal was made."[10] During a controversy over some heretical doctrines, it was Marcella who "took the first steps in getting the heretics condemned. . . . It was she finally who in a succession of letters challenged the heretics to defend themselves."[11] Respect for Marcella was universal in her later years. She died shortly after the sack of Rome in 410.

LATIN MONASTICISM IN THE EAST

What bound these women together was not a formal organization but the ascetic regime they practiced and the ideals they desired. All came from wealthy, pampered backgrounds, and all abandoned the physical trappings of their class. They outdid one another in devotional practices and in acts of charity. Most important, they all shared a love of Scripture and of the intellectual life. With the addition of two more women, the group's involvement in Scripture achieved historical importance. The women became major influences in the lives of key theologians and play a significant role in the history of the church in this century.

These two women were Melanie the Elder (342-ca. 409) and Paula (347-404). Both were wealthy patrician matrons, both were widowed young (Melanie at twenty-two, Paula at thirty-one) with children, and both used their connections, wealth, and leadership qualities to establish renowned monasteries for women and men in the East. Both had as their closest friend a male theologian. While Melanie the Elder worked with Rufinus of Aquileia (345-411) and Paula with Jerome, their contemporaries knew very well that it was the women's money and position that enabled the monasteries to be built and that Melanie the Elder and Paula influenced and directed Rufinus and Jerome respectively as much as vice versa. Even in his scholarly work Jerome acknowledges the hand of Paula pushing him onward. The probing questions of Paula and of her daughter Eustochium concerning scriptural exegesis prompted some of Jerome's most important biblical commentaries.

Melanie the Elder

Melanie the Elder's marriage at age fourteen or fifteen was filled with tragedy. "Besides several miscarriages, which she mourned while her husband was alive, she had the misfortune to lose her husband and two sons within the space of one year, and was left with only one son."[12] These deaths occurred in 364, when she was twenty-two and living in the provinces after her husband's retirement from his prefecture. Momentarily desperate, she returned to Rome within the year and remained there until ca. 372. During her years in Rome Melanie the Elder once again found peace through association with Marcella's Roman circle. Her charity and devotions were well known, but apparently nobody, particularly her family, was prepared for Melanie the Elder's actions in 372. She gave away a large portion of her estates and placed her son and his education under the control of the prefect of the city. Freed from responsibilities that tied her to Rome, she embarked at age thirty on a journey to the East to examine desert asceticism firsthand. Either immediately before or after a six-month pilgrimage to the Nitrian desert she met Rufinus, with whom she formed a relationship that lasted for some twenty years. The two traveled back to Jerusalem around 379-380 and established two monasteries, one for women and one for men, with her money, probably on or near the Mount of Olives. They spent the last twenty-seven years of their lives bestowing "gifts and food on local clergy" and serving "with their own private funds the bishops, solitaires, and virgins who visited them."[13]

The organization of Melanie the Elder's monastery is not known, nor is the rule followed there. Palladius does tell us a bit about Melanie the Elder during her years as a nun, and it is clear she remained a major, if not the major, force in the monastic movement, for "no one failed to benefit by her good works, neither in the east nor in the west, neither in the north nor in the south. For thirty-seven years she practiced hospitality; from her own treasury she made donations to churches, monasteries, guests, and prisons."[14] The relationship between Melanie the Elder and Rufinus is not documented, but we know she became the spiritual director of Evagrius Ponticus (345-399/400), a theologian whose writings are at the heart of

Western monasticism. She was well suited for such direction: "She was most erudite and fond of literature, and she turned night into day going through every writing of the ancient commentators—three million lines of Origen, and a half million lines of Gregory, Stephen, Pieius, Basil and other worthy men. And she did not read them once only or in an offhand way, but she worked on them, dredging through each book seven or eight times."[15] Around 400 Melanie the Elder decided to leave her monastery in Jerusalem and return to Rome, where we can figuratively say she passed her monastic baton to her granddaughter, Melanie the Younger.

Paula

Paula (347-404) lived a very similar life. A patrician by birth, and happily married at age fifteen into another powerful Roman family, she found herself a widow in 379 at age thirty-one, with five children. Instead of remarrying, she became associated with the Roman circle gathered at Marcella's Aventine palace. Paula's daughter Eustochium was as attracted to the group as Paula was and soon moved into the palace to be brought up with other young virgins. Even though Paula frequented the palace, particularly for Scripture study, an area in which she excelled, she did not move there. She maintained her own household and her status as Christian widow. Most of Paula's time was devoted to bringing up her other children, to almsgiving, and to charitable activities. Her reputation as an exemplar Christian widow and avid Scripture student spread far and wide, and her association with Marcella's circle only increased the high regard all held for the women of the Roman circle. When Pope Damasus' call for a council in 382 brought numerous bishops and theologians to Rome, many visitors gained personal knowledge of the circle. Bishop Epiphanus (b. 310), the most venerated elder of the East, stayed with Paula during his winter-long visit. During his visit, her palace filled daily with churchmen from the East and patrician women from Rome, who discussed the ascetic movement they all so loved. Paula's desire to leave her house, family, and possessions for the desert was probably born during this time, but the reality of her family responsibilities made it a dream that had to be postponed.

It was advantageous for the history of female monasticism that Paula remained in Rome, for during the next few years she developed a relationship with Jerome that would lead to her establishment of monasteries in Bethlehem. Jerome had gone to Rome in 382 to defend his friend Paulinus' claim to the see of Antioch before the council. Both men quickly became regular visitors to both Marcella's and Paula's homes. At winter's end the council members returned to the East; Jerome remained in Rome as papal secretary. Marcella and her formidable group at first just asked him for a few lectures on Scripture to further their knowledge, but the group was insatiable in its thirst for biblical scholarship. Soon they were almost harassing Jerome to answer questions on complex passages. Jerome writes of Marcella that "she never met me without asking some questions about [Scripture], nor would she rest content at once, but would bring forward points on the other side; this, however, was not for the sake of argument, but that by questioning she might learn an answer to such objections as she saw might be raised."[16] The nature of the inquiries indicates the high level of scholarship at which these women were operating, as does Jerome's letter to Marcella, where we see her treated as his intellectual equal. "Ask me all the other questions you want when we are alone together. In that way if we happen to show our ignorance, the secret will have neither witness nor judge and will be entombed in a trusty ear."[17]

The Roman circle continued to study with Jerome for the next two years until even the younger generation was fluent in the languages necessary for biblical scholarship: Latin, Greek, and Hebrew. At the funeral of Blesilla, Paula's second oldest daughter, Jerome eulogizes that "had you heard her speak Greek you would have deemed her ignorant of Latin. . . . She even rivaled the great Origen in those acquirements which won for him the admiration of Greece." Furthermore, "in a few months, or rather days, she so completely mastered the difficulties of Hebrew as to emulate her mother's zeal in learning."[18] In December 384, Pope Damasus died, and with him went Jerome's protection against his enemies. Within six months Jerome was ordered by an ecclesiastical court to return to Antioch, which he did. Paula, meanwhile, had been putting her family affairs in order and was ready to fulfill her dream of life in the desert. She set sail for the East in September with her oldest daughter Eustochium, met with Jerome, and then together they proceeded to visit the ascetics in Palestine and in the Nitrian desert. In 386 the three settled in Bethlehem where Paula built two monasteries, one for women and one for men, and later on, a guest house for pilgrims.

Life in the monasteries roughly followed the rules Paula saw observed in Pachomian monasteries in the Nitrian desert. The women were divided into three groups for meals and during work periods. They came together at the third, sixth, and ninth hours, at evening, and in the middle of the night for the singing of the Psalms (*opus Dei*, or Divine Office). On Sunday they all walked to mass, and upon return, they each received their individual work assignments for the week. Servants were not allowed and the women did most of the manual labor—scrubbing floors, tending fires, cooking, serving, sewing—as well as work for the poor. Total obedience to the superior, poverty, detachment, discipline, and charity were the virtues emphasized. Much stress was placed on Scripture. The women daily sang the whole Psalter, which they had to learn by heart, as they did the rest of Scripture.

Paula and Jerome continued to rely on each other for intellectual stimulation. Jerome presented Paula and Eustochium with a translation of Didymus' *Treatise on the Holy Ghost*, and Paula responded with a demand that Jerome translate Origen's homilies on St. Luke for her community—and on and on they would go. One of her requests had an interesting result. Paula insisted that Jerome provide an accurate translation of the Psalter for her monastery. Jerome in turn demanded that his critical work (still the basis for most modern translations) be copied exactly by Paula and Eustochium themselves in their monastery. Here we see the beginning of one of monasticism's most important contributions to Western culture, the monastic scriptorium.

Paula's and Jerome's monasteries acted as beacons throughout the Mediterranean for earnest Christians interested in the new institution of monasticism. From Africa came Alypius, Augustine of Hippo's emissary and dearest friend, to report on Paula's monasteries; from Spain came the wealthy Lucinius who, together with his wife, Theodora, wanted to imitate Bethlehem's monastic experiment in their native land; and from nearby Eleutheropolis came one most dear to Paula's heart, Bishop Epiphanius, the same Epiphanius whose stories so long ago had inspired her to establish the monasteries at Bethlehem. Also came Melanie the Younger (385-448), the granddaughter of Melanie the Elder and the most famous member of the third generation of the Roman circle.

Melanie the Younger

Melanie the Younger's life follows the same pattern as many of the women before her. Of patrician birth, wealthy, married at age fourteen, she had two children who died in childhood. She was not widowed though; she made her husband Pinian promise as she lay dying after giving birth to a son already dead that "if you want me to continue living, give your word before God that we will spend the rest of our lives in chastity."[19] From this extorted promise onward, Pinian was her companion and partner in all her travels, ascetic practices, and monastic foundations.

They started out slowly. First, recognizing "the softness of our way of life,"[20] they decided not to immerse themselves in the rigors of extreme asceticism right away, but instead devoted their energies to the poor, the imprisoned, and those in debt. Next, they gave away all of their Roman possessions and used the proceeds to found and endow monasteries for monks and virgins. When the Gothic invasion forced the couple and Melanie's mother, Albina, to flee to their estates first in Sicily in 408 and then in northern Africa in 410, they finally began living the ascetic life. They settled near Thagaste so they could be near Augustine's friend Alypius, the town's bishop and a renowned scholar. They built and endowed two monasteries there, one for 60 men, the other for 130 women. There Melanie the Younger lived a rigorous and scholarly life. She copied the Old and New Testament, recited the divine office by heart, devoured all books "that were bought, as well as those she chanced upon," [21] be they in Latin or Greek, and was repeatedly called out of her solitude to teach others.

Seven years after settling in Africa, the three moved on to Jerusalem. They left Jerusalem briefly for a tour of the Egyptian desert, and when they returned the second time they settled there permanently, living an "ascetic regime for fourteen years"[22] until Albina's death in 431. Melanie the Younger, then in her mid-forties, brought her mother's remains to the Mount of Olives, near where Melanie the Elder had her monastery. After a period of mourning Melanie the Younger "had a monastery built for herself," other virgins, and "women from places of ill-repute" in 432.[23] The monastery housed ninety women, and after Pinian's death, Melanie built a chapel, a church, and a monastery for men in 436. The women chanted the office at the third, sixth, and ninth hours, evening, and the middle of the night. On feasts and Sundays the women would "chant something beyond the customary office."[24] An oratory in the monastery allowed the women to attend mass on Fridays and Sundays. Fasting was allowed but by "everybody's own personal decision"[25] because "of all the virtues, fasting is the least."[26] Obedience was exalted as "the greatest possession"[27] and given not only to the superior but to each other.

During Melanie the Younger's lifetime these monasteries were famous throughout Christian lands for their learning and piety, and "many of the wives of senators and some of the men illustrious in learning" visited often so they could "investigate the orthodox faith" with Melanie the Younger. "And she, who had the Holy Spirit in dwelling, did not cease talking theology from dawn to dusk."[28] The empress Eudocia, wife of Theodosius II, went to visit Melanie the Younger and her monastery in 438 and called Melanie "my mother."[29] With Melanie the Younger's death in 439 the sources for the Bethlehem community disappear.

NATIVE FORMS OF MONASTICISM IN THE EAST

Macrina

The Roman circle and its satellite groups in the Holy Land were not the only groups participating in the formation of female monasticism in this crucial period. Macrina the Younger (330-379) was born into one of the most brilliant and sainted families in Christianity's history. Macrina the Elder was her grandmother; Emmelia was her mother; Basil the Great, Peter, and Gregory of Nyssa were her brothers; and all are honored in the church as saints. Everything we know about the family indicates that Macrina was its spiritual center. When "the great Basil returned after his long period of education . . . he was puffed up beyond measure" with his success in the world. This is when Macrina "took him in hand," as mentioned earlier, "and with such speed did she draw him also" to the ascetic life and an intense Christian faith. Peter was "always looking to his sister as the model of all good," because in fact Melanie "reared him herself," becoming "all things to the boy: father, teacher, attendant, mother." When Gregory visited his sister on her deathbed, it was he who asked for comfort and advice, while "never did she even look for help" from him, even in her last hours. And in the later years of her mother's life, Macrina became her guide and led her on to "this philosophic and spiritual manner of life."[30]

Macrina persuaded her mother to turn the household into a model of familial monasticism where all lived "on a footing of equality with the staff of maids" in an atmosphere permeated by humility, poverty, asceticism, and piety. Women from the surrounding area were drawn to the household, and "their successes increased with the lapse of time."[31] Peter and Basil were especially supportive of the community, as were friends Gregory of Nazianzus (330-390) and Eustathius, bishop of Sebaste (300-377). After Emmelia's death the community took on a more definitive monastic form, and by the time of Gregory's visit in Macrina's last hours it was well established with a church of its own and a male community on the opposite side of the river. The women in this double monastery (a female monastery with a male monastery that ministers to the women and usually is under one authority) were presided over by Macrina; the men, by Peter—the same brother whose spiritual mother was Macrina. Plainly it was Macrina who was the guiding spirit in the monastic settlement.

Gregory of Nyssa's vivid description of the number and the emotional state of those who participated in Macrina's funeral procession makes her exalted status throughout the countryside exceedingly clear. At one point he wondered whether the burial services would ever by completed "for the crowds that came with us and those that were constantly joining us"[32] slowed them down so considerably. The sources do not tell us whether Peter's and Macrina's double monastery followed one of their brother Basil's popular monastic rules (*Long Rules* and *Short Rules*), and we have no direct evidence in the sources acknowledging Macrina's influence on the shape Basil gave his rules. It will suffice to reiterate the facts as known: Macrina was the spiritual mother of the family, including Basil; Macrina fashioned a familial monasticism in the family estate for her mother, herself, and their household; Basil's Rules envision monasticism as "a spiritual family living under one roof, a kind of house-monastery."[33]

The Rule of St. Augustine

The great Augustine of Hippo also wrote a monastic rule. While it was one of the most popular rules during the High Middle Ages and Early Modern periods, its impact on female monasticism in the centuries immediately following its composition was slight. Still, the circumstances surrounding its origin provide evidence that women were involved in monasticism during its formative stage in northern Africa and that they were perceived to be integral members of monasticism. Augustine came into contact with Marcella's Roman monastic groups when he traveled to Rome in 383. After his baptism in 385 he desired to imitate such monastic groups, and so soon he set up a similar communal group at his estate in Thagaste. When Augustine was made bishop of Hippo, he turned the episcopal house into a monastery. In 410 Augustine was still very much concerned about monasticism; when Melanie the Younger and Pinian settled in northern Africa and decided to give away all their African property, Augustine advised them not just to found a monastery but "give both a house and an income to each monastery"[34] so that it could survive.

Augustine's sister was part of the monastic movement and was a superior of a monastery in Hippo. After her death a dispute arose among the nuns about the organization of life within the monastery. Augustine, with personal knowledge of his sister's community, responded with a letter detailing his conception of monastic life. This letter, in an amended form, is what future generations call the *Rule of St. Augustine*.

Olympias

Olympias (361-408), too often known only as the friend of John Chrysostom (344-407), was as important to women's religious life in Constantinople as Marcella was in Rome. Her life followed the same pattern as her Roman counterpart. Born into a powerful patrician family, exceedingly wealthy in her own right after her parents' deaths, she was left a childless widow in 386 at age twenty-five after a two-year marriage to Nebridius, prefect of Constantinople. She decided against remarriage (her rejection of Emperor Theodosius' relative resulted in her property being impounded for five years) and was ordained a deaconess by Nectatius, bishop of Constantinople, soon after being widowed. Before long she had a group of patrician women meeting in her home for spiritual discussions and to organize charitable works.

Her friendship with John Chrysostum, made bishop of Constantinople in 398, grew during the years into almost a partnership, particularly in almsgiving. Olympias had the money and the desire, while John had the common sense necessary in the administration of such large-scale charity: "Perceiving that she bestowed her goods liberally on any who asked her for them," John advised her to "regulate your donations according to the wants of those who solicit relief."[35] John placed numerous widows and virgins under Olympias' care, for whom she built a monastery next to the cathedral. Called Olympiados, it housed 250 nuns. She also built a home for the sick and an orphanage there.

Eventually her friendship and loyalty to John cost Olympias her monastery and charitable houses, for when John was sent into exile during a conflict with the imperial party, his friends also paid a price. Olympias was first accused of setting the fire of 404 that destroyed St. Sophia and many public buildings, then she was forced into exile for not acknowledging John's illegitimate successor, and finally she had to watch her community and charitable houses be disbanded. Even from exile she commanded respect and retained her position as monastic leader of women and trusted friend of John. It was with Olympias that John entrusted his very well-being: "Now, once more, I trust to your prudence and discretion as to my future dwelling place."[36] She lived long enough to see peace restored in the church in Constantinople and her monastery reestablished, and, since her death at the age of forty-seven, "those who live at Constantinople number her among the confessors."[37]

2

Women Religious in the Early Medieval West

One of the pilgrims who visited the Holy Land between 381 and 384, the years in which Melanie the Elder was establishing her monastery, was a woman known as Egeria (also known as Etheria or Silvia). Egeria was the superior of a religious community located somewhere on the Atlantic coast, probably Aquitania or Galicia, and visited the Holy Land so she could better instruct her community and understand Scripture. "I want you to be quite clear about these mountains, reverend ladies my sisters," Egeria wrote as she described Mt. Sinai. "I know it has been rather a long business writing down all these places one after the other, and it makes far too much to remember. But it may help you, loving sisters, the better to picture what happened in these places when you read the holy Books of Moses."[1] We know, then, that Egeria practiced asceticism in a communal setting and saw the study of Scripture as necessary and beneficial to her community's spiritual life. We also know that even women north of the Mediterranean were pursuing goals similar to those of the Roman circle by the late fourth century.

Egeria is one of the few women who lived in a religious community in the West in Late Antiquity that we can identify by name. Many times we know nothing more than their existence. There was, for example, one community of twenty women in Bologna that was bound by a common rule and was self-supporting. Ambrose tells us about a similar community in Verona. The first male monastic communities the sources mention are associated with Martin of Tours (316-397). He first established a monastery in Milan, then one on the island of Gallinaria, then another at Ligugé, and, finally, one outside of Tours where he began the monastery of Marmoutier in 372. There may have been a community of women associated with Martin's male monasteries; the sources are not clear.

A monastery for men ruled by brothers Romanus (400-ca. 463) and Lupicinus (d. 480) and a monastery for women, Beaume les Dames, ruled by their sister were founded in the Jura region near Lake Geneva during the mid-fifth century. Romanus was buried at the women's monastery at his request because "I do not want to have my tomb in a monastery which women are forbidden to enter."[2] John Cassian (365-435), author of *Institutes* and *Conferences*, two of the most influential texts in Western monasticism, founded two monasteries in Marseilles. One he ruled, and one his sister ruled, the monastery of the Holy Savior.

IRELAND

In Ireland the sources are slightly more abundant. Patrick (397?-461) tells us that "sons of the Irish and daughters of their underkings were monks and virgins of Christ—I cannot count their number."[3] He is especially impressed by the resilience of women in their pursuit of the ascetic life: "They endure persecution and their own parents' unfair reproaches, and yet their number grows larger and larger . . . not to mention widows and the self-denying. But it is the women kept in slavery who suffer especially; they even have to endure constant threats and terrorisation. . . . "[4] Because of such opposition it was rare for a woman to live as a consecrated virgin in her paternal home. The norm was for women to live together on land possessed by missionaries and to perform services for the church—make vestments, clean interiors of churches, catechize children, and the like. Brigid of Kildare (ca. 456-524/25), the co-patron saint of Ireland along with Patrick, is remembered as the person most responsible for the spread of female monasticism in Ireland. Brigid instilled in the female communities of her day a discipline, organization, and spirit that would remain characteristic of Irish monasticism for centuries.

Unfortunately, the surviving vitae of Brigid are lean on facts, so only the barest outline of her life is known. She was born of noble parents (or at least a noble father) in Conaille Muirtheimhne and was well educated. She refused to marry when her parents so requested and instead took a vow of chastity before Bishop Maccaille, a disciple of Patrick. In the years that followed, her personality, education, and holiness attracted so many men and women that she founded the great monastery of Kildare, "head of almost all the churches of Ireland and overtopping (like a mountain peak) all the monasteries of the Irish."[5] Brigid's biographer describes it as somewhat similar to a double monastery. The women shared a common rule and a church with the men, but each monastery was autonomous. The men gave obedience to a bishop, the women to an abbess. They had separate entrances to the church, and the church had a high partition running down its length to keep each side hidden from the sight of the other.

As Brigid's reputation grew, demand for her direction increased and led to numerous monastic foundations for women throughout Ireland. She provided the monasteries with a rule, but it is not extant. Her contemporaries praised her charitable acts and hospitality, but it was her scholarship that impressed them the most. Her wisdom was sought after by the "most eminent persons"; Brendan of Clonfert (486-575) supposedly asked her for instructions "on a certain religious subject."[6] On occasion she exercised the clerical function of preaching to men, and she has the distinction of being the only known woman to be consecrated a bishop, albeit through an error. Her monasteries educated the women within and probably also the girls in the surrounding area.

Brigid was the most famous female leader of her day, but not the only one. Moninne (d. 518?), also called Darerca, was a contemporary of Brigid. Her biographer tells us she received the veil from the hands of the aged Patrick himself. At first closely associated with the community of virgins Patrick had gathered around himself, Moninne soon struck out on her own. She formed a community in Leinster and placed it under the authority of a bishop. Facing discord between the community and the bishop, and clergy jealous of her popularity, Moninne prudently decided to leave Leinster. She and a group of fifty women moved north to Sliab Cuilinn, where Moninne established a noted and respected monastery.

Often called "the Brigid of the North," Ita (d. ca. 570) was another formidable leader, the founder of the first known monastery in western Ireland. After overcoming parental opposition Ita made a vow of virginity and received the veil. She traveled to Corcu Oche and founded a monastery at Cluain-Credhuil. An integral part of its fame was its school for boys. So many future church leaders were educated in Ita's school that she also is known as the foster mother of the saints of Ireland. Her monastery and school were guided by a simple yet profound dictum: "True faith in God with purity of heart; simplicity of life with religion; generosity with charity."[7]

Sources briefly mention other women and monasteries, enough for us at least to know of their existence and success. Cairech Dergan, for example, founded a famous monastery in Rosecommon sometime before 578; the sources tell us no more. Nevertheless, significant facts can be deduced from these lean sources. We know that female monasteries supported themselves largely through farming their lands. The women did not do the farming themselves, as did the monks. Therefore, the women actually had more experience as administrators. They had to manage a rather large complex: hire laborers, rent to tenants, maintain farm animals and equipment, and so on. In agriculture, as in the intellectual life and in education, these Irish nuns exercised extensive powers.

SPAIN

We have already mentioned that one married couple, Lucinus and Theodora, went to Paula and Jerome's monasteries for advice on how to establish a monastery in their native Spain, but we know nothing more than that. Even if we assume that they did begin a monastery and that it succeeded, it would be the only one noted in known sources of Late Antiquity. The presence of groups of virgins is noted in council canons, but the reason they are mentioned is because they were so loosely structured and disorganized. The only communities for women that are known to have thrived are those formed by the aristocratic followers of Priscillian (ca. 340-ca. 386), a condemned bishop who preached rigorous asceticism. Orthodox, organized monasticism is not mentioned in known sources until the sixth century.

During the course of that century double monasteries apparently were founded throughout Spain, for in 619 the Council of Seville dealt with the question of regulating the relationship between monks and nuns in well-established monasteries. The monks administered the monasteries and cared for all secular concerns. The women's property was separate from the men's, and the women made the men's clothes. Double monasteries in Spain, though, were of a specific nature. More than any other territory, Spain fostered monastic communities composed of whole families. Father and son entered the men's monastery, while mother and daughter entered the women's. In the mid-seventh century Fructuous (d. 665) ruled one of these double or family monasteries called Nono in a desert between Seville and Cadiz. He wrote two monastic rules, the first for men only, but the second one for these family monasteries. The rule sets forth instructions on how, when, and where the men and women, sisters and brothers, parents and children, may have contact and how to maintain a spirit of chastity within the monastery.

MEROVINGIAN GAUL

During the years the Merovingian dynasty ruled the Franks—from the fifth to the seventh century—female monastic communities in Merovingian Gaul enjoyed particular prominence, respect, and success probably more than at any time prior to the High Middle Ages. Rules specifically for female communities written at this time (four complete rules and fragments of possibly three more survived), legislated certain features that these communities were to retain for the next millennium. Such concentrated effort to provide structure and guidance for women's communities indicate that society deemed it beneficial to institutionalize a communal life for women. While the contributions of women's communities were recognized as valuable and worthy of full support, it also was realized that problems peculiar to women's communities had to be addressed.

Caesarius of Arles' Rule for Nuns

The first written monastic rule exclusively for women that has survived was penned by Caesarius of Arles (470-542) between 512 and 534. Caesarius and Caesaria, brother and sister, were both enthusiasts of monastic life. When Caesarius was made bishop of Arles in 502, he was in a position to provide his sister with an opportunity to head her own monastery by building one "to adorn the church of Arles."[8] Caesaria had "learn[ed] what she must teach" about monastic life during her stay at the monastery of the Holy Savior in Marseilles. She assumed leadership of a fledgling group of three or four when the monastery of St. John was dedicated in 512. Caesarius "at the beginning of the foundation of the monastery" wrote a rule for them, and during the next twenty-two years the women were to "determine by diligent experiment" what parts were "in harmony with reason and possibility and sanctity."[9] It is Caesarius, therefore, who asks all to remember that the rule is the result of a collaborative effort between himself and the women.

During the reign of Caesaria and her successor, Caesaria the Younger, as abbess, the monastery grew and prospered. Before his death in 542 Caesarius handed over complete control of the monastery to Caesaria the Younger, his sister having predeceased him. The monastery's fame as an ecclesiastical center and a repository for a women's monastic rule continued to grow well into the next century.

The *Rule for Nuns*, like almost all rules written during the Early Middle Ages, was more derivative than original. "The prescriptions of the ancient Fathers" are included in the rule, and the rest is inspired by the *Rule of St. Augustine* and John Cassian's works.[10] Traditionally commentators have maintained that the most original aspect of the rule was the establishment of strict enclosure, but, in fact, a review of previous practices of women's — and men's — communities indicates that such living arrangements were already known. In the desert Pachomian monasteries for women demanded a rigorous enclosure, and Abbot Isidore's monastery for men would accept only those monks who would agree to absolute enclosure "until death."[11] Paula's nuns were allowed to go to Sunday liturgy as a community, but at all other times "so strictly did Paula separate them from men that she would not allow even eunuchs to approach them."[12] Melanie the Younger's community had to maintain complete segregation from men, and she had a chapel built within the monastery so the women did not have to leave the building for liturgy. And in Gaul when a woman entered the monastery of Beaume les Dames, "she was never again seen on the outside, except at her death."[13]

Once we dismiss the question of originality, we are still left with two questions: Why is enclosure in the *Rule for Nuns* so significant, and why does enclosure increase in importance during the next centuries, so much so that it eventually becomes an identifying feature of late female medieval monasticism? There are many possible answers. Enclosure was a way of eliminating distractions and insuring an atmosphere conducive to the contemplative life, monasticism's true goal. Enclosure prevented infiltration of worldly problems. A woman could not manage her property or inheritance from a monastery without being distracted; enclosure made sure she was not distracted by eliminating the temptation to manage her affairs actively. By allowing only certain men to enter (clergy, workmen, slaves, relatives) under regulated conditions, the women protected their reputations. Enclosure forbade *convivia* — banquet dinners for important people and relatives customarily given by female communities — to all but fellow female religious; such legislation focused the nun inwardly both physically and mentally. With only necessary and minimal contact with powerful people, the chance of interference was greatly reduced. Enclosure was a logical way of offering separation from the world to women whose monastery was not a castlelike building in the wilderness but an ordinary house inside the city walls. It also was thought to give women a bit more security in times of invasions. (St. John's in Arles was first started outside the city, destroyed by the Goths, and then rebuilt inside the city walls with enclosure.) In addition, in the beginning the monastic lives of men and women were almost indistinguishable. Only after the differences were increased and legislated does enclosure become more associated with women than with men. But the growth of differences between male and female monasticism may in turn be due to the response each sex made to societal needs. The sixth century was a century of invasions, changes in political power centers and transitory culture. Male monasticism responded to these new needs with a vow of stability (the solemn promise to remain in the same monastery for life), female monasticism with enclosure, which in turn guaranteed stability.

Enclosure was mandated by papal bull in the thirteenth century, but there is no linear development from the *Rule for Nuns* to the universal requirement of enclosure. The rule probably was responsible for the presence of many enclosed monasteries by the time the Council of Orleans met in 549 and mentioned them. On the other hand, when Donatus of Besançon (fl. 627-658) used the *Rule for Nuns* as a major source in his rule for his mother's monastery in the seventh century, he tempered enclosure for monasteries in rural areas.

Even though the *Rule for Nuns* did not exercise great influence in its own world (only one convent adopted it in toto in the sixth century), it is of interest to the historian for reasons other than the issue of enclosure. It presents us with a detailed picture of female monasticism. Equality in the *Rule for Nuns* began in poverty, at the moment of entrance; no one could be received "unless beforehand they deed over, or give, or sell, to whomsoever they wish, all their possessions."[14] Literacy is required and intellectual activity must occupy the women at least two hours a day. While the community does manual labor together in the morning one nun must read aloud to them. Books were so essential to their life that one of the offices of the community was that of librarian. A school was maintained in the monastery where girls six years or older were taught. They all, except abbess and prioress, took turns at cooking and washing, and did whatever jobs were assigned to them. They made their own clothing, and that clothing could not be quilted, embroidered, or dyed, but had to be plain or milk-white color. Bedrooms were communal, simple and undecorated, and silver could not be used for dining. Discipline was enforced and obedience demanded, even as to how high women tied up their hair. Recitation of the Office was to occupy them most of the day and was complemented by constant recollection. Fasting was required during much of the year, but after observing the community's "strength or possibility," the abbess was to "endeavor to make regulations" regarding how to fast.[15]

Radegund

As mentioned, only one other monastery, Holy Cross, is known to have adopted the *Rule for Nuns* in its original form. Holy Cross Monastery was founded by Radegund, one of the most beloved leaders of Merovingian times and certainly the best-documented woman of the era. Thanks to the inherent drama of her life and to the times, and the literary skills of her three biographers — Venantius Fortunatus, Baudonivia, and Gregory of Tours — the vitae of Radegund are well known and have served to increase her fame throughout the ages.

Radegund, daughter of Thuringian king Bertechar, was born during the turbulent second decade of the sixth century. When twelve years old she was won in war by Clotaire I and taken to Athies, a royal villa, to be educated. At age eighteen she was married to him. Childless, Radegund spent her free time in charitable works: "She built a house at Athies where beds were elegantly made up for needy women gathered there. She would wash them herself in warm baths, tending to the putrescence of their diseases. She washed the heads of men, acting like a servant."[16] For six years husband and wife tolerated each other: Clotaire, her ascetic practices; Radegund, his infidelities. When Clotaire murdered her brother Radegund retired (or was retired) from the court. She then brazenly got the bishop of Noyon to consecrate her as a deaconess. Next she went to a royal villa in Poitou, where her apostolate among the needy extended to lepers. The real Radegund can be seen working here. After kissing a leper, a servant "presumed to chide her softly, 'Most holy lady, when you have embraced lepers, who will kiss you?' Pleasantly, she answered, 'Really, if you won't kiss me, it's no concern of mine.'"[17]

Radegund's retreat was broken by Clotaire's threat to demand her back as wife. Not only was he eventually dissuaded of such action, but he actually was persuaded, probably around 555 to 560, to help Radegund build a monastery. It was during this time that Radegund wrote to Caesaria the Younger for a copy of the *Rule for Nuns*.

There is strong evidence that Radegund's foundation was a double monastery. The women's monastery was called Holy Cross, the men's was St. Mary. Under Radegund's guiding spirit (she declined the office of abbess, "reserving no authority of her own"[18]), the monastery became a political and intellectual as well as spiritual center. "She was always solicitous for peace and worked diligently for the welfare of the fatherland. . . . And she taught us also to pray incessantly for [the kings'] stability. Whenever she heard of bitterness arising among them, trembling, she sent such letters to one and then to the other pleading that they should not make war. . . ."[19] She had a seemingly unquenchable thirst for reading, and she encouraged the nuns to question her about works they did not understand. One of Radegund's biographers was Baudonivia, a learned member of the community. Baudonivia's work makes significant contributions to hagiography by introducing into the genre virtuous practices most often associated with women, such as care for the sick and poor. The monastery possessed relatively high standards of literary endeavor. The nuns may have produced small dramas and written popular songs, but the sources are open to interpretation. The monastery also ran a school for children.

Unfortunately, after Radegund's death the monastery was not peaceful, and within a few years it experienced a scandalous rebellion. Gregory of Tours' detailed narration allows us to view the darker side of women's monasticism. A discontented nun named Chrodield, daughter of King Charibert, "gathered to herself . . . murderers, sorcerers, adulterers, runaway slaves and men guilty of all other crimes. And so she gave them orders to break into the monastery at night and drag the abbess from it . . . to cleave her in two with a sword." Other nuns heard the break-in and tried to come to the abbess's rescue. In the ensuing battle "the men came with drawn swords and spears . . . and seized the prioress instead of the abbess . . . and carried her off to place her under guard at St. Hillary's church" where another leader of the rebellion, Basina, was in charge. With morning light the rebels realized their mistake and planned a second raid at twilight. They returned and this time burned down the storehouse and plundered the monastery. The bishop then got involved, but succeeded only in exasperating the situation. Basina next repented her role in the rebellion and joined forces with the abbess against Chrodield. "Scarcely a day passed without a murder" until Gregory called in Count Macco and his armed retainers to "forcibly put down" the rebellion. Chrodield saw she was outnumbered and surrendered. Her haughty surrender—"Do no violence to me . . . lest a time may come for me to take vengeance on you"—merely infuriated the throng, who proceeded to grab the rebels and "tied them to the stake and beat them fiercely and cut off the hair of some, the hands of others, and in a good many cases the ears and nose, and the rebellion was crushed and there was peace."[20]

Surprisingly, Chrodield and Basina were allowed to present to the bishops their reasons for rebelling. "They asserted that they could not endure any longer the risk of starvation, nakedness, and above all of beating; and they added that several men had bathed in their bath contrary to decency, and that the abbess played games, and that worldly persons dined with her, and that a betrothal had actually taken place in the monastery; that she had impiously made a dress for her niece out of a silk altar cloth . . . and that she had a masquerade in the monastery." Their chief charge, though, was that "she had a man in the monastery who wore woman's clothes . . . and that he was in constant attendance on the abbess herself." The abbess was able to talk her way out of all the charges, and the rebels were excommunicated. So ends the most well- known women's rebellion in the Early Middle Ages. [21]

THE ERA OF DOUBLE MONASTERIES

We have noted the existence of double monasteries numerous times so far in this history. In the seventh century, however, we see the foundations of double monasteries increase significantly, so it might be beneficial to offer a fuller definition of the double monastery before proceeding. A double monastery is not one in which men and women live together in one monastery; that would be a mixed monastery. Nor is a double monastery one in which a women's monastery has juridical ties with, is founded by, or is simply next to a male monastery; each of these would be more properly called an affiliated or adjacent monastery. A double monastery must have one feature in order to qualify: The men's monastery must have priests who minister to the spiritual needs of those in the women's monastery.

Because the men were there to serve the women, the women's superior was also the superior of the men, although this rule of thumb is more true in certain areas and times than in others. In England the abbess ruled the men and women in all the known double monasteries. On the continent there are exceptions to this rule. Some abbesses ruled both houses; some did not. But there is no record of an abbot completely dominating the women's monastery, so one generalization can be made without any known exceptions: Double monasteries benefited women and were responsible in large part for the high visibility and power many women experienced during the seventh century. In England and Gaul especially, women had wide access to the culture of the day and participated in its formation. And double monasteries gave women control over their lives in ways that no other institution at the time was able to do.

It is not difficult to trace the beginning of this brief but productive phenomenon. It mirrors and contributes to the overall increase of activity in women's monasticism. In Gaul (modern France and Belgium), 28.9

percent of all new monasteries founded in the seventh century were for women, and in England, 35.7 percent were.[22] The growth in women's monasticism was in part due to a surge in royal patronage, encouragement by church hierarchy, and the availability of new monastic rules. The rule of Benedict of Nursia (480-550), known as the *Rule of St. Benedict*, was disseminating slowly throughout the continent, but it was not widely used by women until the ninth century. In the seventh century women had a variety of monastic rules specifically for them from which they could choose. By the beginning of the seventh century all urban centers in central Gaul and most in northern Gaul had a women's monastery, and with the spread of double monasteries, northern rural areas had them also. The impetus for the double monastery came from Columbanus' disciples. Columbanus (ca. 540-ca. 615) was an Irish missionary who established a strict monastery first at Annegray, ca. 590 and then at Luxeuil, where he wrote a monastic rule. He never founded any double monasteries himself, but his disciples took his conception of monastic life and worked with women to bring about a vital type of double monastery.

The greatest concentration of double monasteries was in northeast Gaul (Belgium) in Marchiennes, Hamay, Nivelle, Hasnon, Vienne, Maubeuge, Chasteaulieu, Tuffe, Soissons, Troyes, Montierender, Fecamp, Troclare, Chamaliers, and Pacilly. Three double monasteries near Paris—Brie, Chelles, and Andalys—were more influential and well known than the rest, principally because of the reputation their schools and scholars enjoyed, as Bede in his all-important *History of the English Church and People* tells us:

> [King Earconbert's] daughter Earcongota, who shared her father's zeal, was a nun of outstanding virtue, who served God in a convent in Frankish territory founded by the noble Abbess Fara at a place called Brie: for as yet there were few monasteries built in English territory, and many who wished to enter conventual life went from Britain to the Frankish realm of Gaul for the purpose. Girls of noble family were also sent there for their education, or to be betrothed to their heavenly Bridegroom, especially to the houses of Brie, Chelles and Andalys....[23]

Bede provided more bits of information about Brie: Two Anglo-Saxon noblewomen were abbesses there; the "brethren of the monastery who lived in separate buildings"[24] from the women were under the abbess's authority; and the men shared the church with the women.

Both Andalys and Chelles were founded originally by Frankish queen Clotilda, wife of Clovis I, in the sixth century. Chelles was revived by Queen Bathilda (d. ca. 679), a woman of outstanding abilities. After being captured in England and made a slave, she was sold to the mayor of Neustria as a chambermaid. Before long she was noticed by the king, Clovis II, and they married. When Clovis II died in 658 she began her second career as nun and monastic benefactor. "She showered great estates and whole forests upon [religious communities] for the construction of their cells and monasteries. And at Chelles, in the region of Paris, she built a great community of virgins as her own special house of God. There she established the maiden Bertilla" as its first abbess. She joined the community herself but continued to grant "many great estates to the basilicas of the saints and monasteries of the city of Paris," so many that to "give an account of all the blessings she conferred is utterly beyond our power." She even endowed the basilicas of Peter and Paul in Rome with gifts and gave to the poor in that city. Bathilda demanded that those living the monastic life remain virtuous, particularly the men: "She would send orders and letters warning bishops and abbots that the monks dwelling in those places ought to live according to their holy rule and order." Never forgetting her own background, she showed deep concern about the slave trade in the realm and often ransomed the captives. She then placed "the captives she released and other people in monasteries, particularly as many men and women of her own people as possible and cared for them."[25]

Bathilda's choice of Bertilla as abbess of Chelles helped the monastery grow, for as Bertilla's reputation as a prudent ruler spread "even more men and women hastened to her, not only from neighboring provinces but even from across the seas."[26] One of the Anglo-Saxon women who joined Chelles was Herewith, remembered chiefly as the sister of Hilda (614-680), the most accomplished and powerful Anglo-Saxon abbess of the medieval period. When Hilda "decided to abandon the secular life and serve God alone, she went to the province of the East Angles . . . to travel on from there to Gaul, and to live in exile for our Lord's sake in the monastery of Chelles . . . for her sister was already living there as a professed nun. . . . Inspired by her example Hilda remained in the province a full year, intending to join her overseas." Hilda lingered too long, though, and was recalled by a bishop and instructed to observe on some land he donated "the monastic rule with a handful of companions for another year. After this [ca. 650] Hilda was made abbess of the monastery of Hartlepool," a double monastery, where she stayed for seven years. Next, "she further undertook to found or organize a monastery at a place known as Streanreshalch [Whitby]."[27]

Whitby grew in number, stature, and political importance under her leadership. Bede tells us "five men from this monastery later became bishops," that "so great was her prudence that not only ordinary folk but kings and princes used to come and ask her advice," and that all members of the monastery were "required to make a thorough study of the Scriptures."[28] In recognition of Hilda's leadership role in the English church, the hierarchy and nobility chose to hold the most important council of the Anglo-Saxon period, the Synod of 663, at her monastery.

Whitby and Hilda were not exceptions. Many other women ruled double monasteries and were acknowledged throughout the land as leaders in the English church. Hilda's successor attended a church council in 704 and was sought after by the archbishop of Canterbury for advice. Ethelthrith ruled from Ely, Eanswith from Folkstone (probably the earliest women's monastery in England, founded ca. 630), Sexburga from Sheppy, Ethelburga from Barking, Eormenbeorg from Minster-in-Thanet, and Cuthburga from Wimborne. All these women were of strong, independent character and ruled both men and women. Their monasteries were centers of study where schools, libraries, and scriptoria thrived. The women under their authority were expected to know ancient law, history, allegory, chronography, grammar, orthography, punctuation, and the writings of Cassian and Gregory the Great. They made clothes and vestments. Abbesses taught younger nuns poetry. While the women were segregated from the men, they came together as a community for certain ceremonies, such as burials. Some of these women even made pilgrimages to Rome and were missionaries in Germany. All of this, unfortunately, came to an end during the Viking invasions of the late eighth and the ninth centuries. Before double monasteries disappeared, though, mention should be made of two more of these women who made their mark on German history.

Germany had only two double monasteries to boast of, but they and their abbesses were highly honored throughout the medieval period. Lioba was a nun at the double monastery of Minster-in-Thanet in the early eighth century when she wrote a letter to a distant relative, the famous Boniface (672/74-754). Boniface, an Anglo-Saxon missionary, was commissioned by Pope Gregory II in 718 and again in 722 to convert the peoples of Frisia, Hesse, Thuringia, and Bavaria. His accomplishments had impressed Christians throughout the West, including Lioba, so she wrote and introduced herself, using the pretense of needing him "to correct the unskilled style of this letter and to send one, by way of example, a few kind words." This first glimpse of Lioba reveals an earnest, eager, ambitious woman who wanted "to exercise my little talents" so much that she approached even a prestigious stranger for help.[29] Boniface was touched, and the letter marks the beginning of a lifelong relationship that ends with Boniface's ultimate tribute: It was "his words that after his death her bones should be placed next to him in the tomb, so that they who had served God during their lifetime with equal sincerity and zeal await together the day of resurrection."[30]

The change in their relationship from correspondents to partners began after Boniface asked the monasteries of Minster-in-Thanet and Wimborne for volunteers to help him in his missionary work. Lioba enthusiastically responded to Boniface's call. She led a group of Anglo Saxon women across the channel and set to work establishing mission stations that she eventually would turn into monasteries. Two women, Chunihildt and Berthgit, ran a school in Thuringia, another woman named Thecla became abbess first at Kitzingen and then at Ochsenfurt, while Lioba became abbess at the double monastery of Tauberbischofsheim. Lioba's biographer tells us how her amicable nature and fair rule won the hearts of all and helped spread the network of missionaries throughout the countryside. Continuing in the tradition of Anglo-Saxon double monasteries, she gave education high priority, so much so that "she and all the sisters under her rule went to rest after the midday meal and she would never give permission to any of them to stay up late, for she said that the lack of sleep dulled the mind, especially for study."[31] Boniface trusted her decisions explicitly and in advance: "Be assured, therefore, that whatever you may see fit to do in this matter . . . shall have our consent and approval."[32]

Lioba was an effective worker. She made complete surveys of possible locations for her monasteries and anticipated possible problems and solutions. The settlements were at first just huts built near the people they were trying to convert in the rural areas. Lioba and her nuns worked alongside the monks in their joint missionary venture. Slowly they replaced the huts with permanent buildings—monasteries, churches, and schools. They went to great lengths to learn the local dialect; the monks needed it for preaching, and the nuns needed it for teaching. The nuns also maintained hospitals where they dispensed medicine and food and hostels where they sheltered travelers and guests.

Only one other double monastery is known to exist in Germany at this time, the monastery of Heidenheim. The Anglo-Saxon woman Walburga (710-779) was a distant relative of both Lioba and Boniface. When her father and two brothers, Wunibald and Willibald, decided to make a pilgrimage to the Holy Land when she was ten years old, she asked if she could attend the monastery school at Wimborne while they were gone. She did, and she excelled in all subjects. Upon her father's death when she was seventeen (possibly twenty), she made a permanent commitment to monastic life. When she was thirty, Boniface wrote Wimborne and made a plea for more volunteers to assist him in the missionary fields. Walburga left England for the continent with a group of forty nuns. Following a three-week hike from the coast to Thuringia, the group split into three, each group going to train at one of the three monasteries Lioba had set up for that purpose. Walburga inherited the rule of the abbey of Heidenheim upon her brother Wunibald's death on December 19, 761. (German custom allowed monastic rule to be passed on within one's family.) By year's end she and a number of Anglo-Saxon nuns moved into the abbey and made it a double monastery. Using her knowledge of the governance of double monasteries at Wimborne, she quickly had a thriving institution. Walburga taught Latin, Greek, mathematics, botany, literature, and music to the children of the region in Heidenheim's school, as she had been taught at Wimborne. When she died in 799 her other brother Willibald became abbot and Heidenheim probably ceased to be a double monastery.

3

Restriction and Revival

The seventh century was indeed a fortuitious era in female religious life. The power and respect of Anglo-Saxon abbesses in their society marks a high point not only in monastic history but in the history of Western women in general. In Frankish territory women religious were as respected as their Anglo-Saxon counterparts, although they were not quite as active politically. In Ireland Brigid's successors at the monastery of Kildare continued to hold a unique position of prominence and authority in the governance of the church. In Italy women's communities were small but their abbesses were autonomous. For various reasons—lack of strong political structures, the popularity of asceticism, the decentralization of ecclesiastical organization—the spiritual equality of women was perceived more easily in this century than at other times, and this allowed women greater access to the intellectual and cultural life of their society. And since the female monasteries of the period were not limited to the ruling class but admitted women of all classes (recall Queen Bathilda's admission of redeemed captives to her monasteries), the impact of these institutions was felt throughout the whole of society.

RESTRICTION

This golden age of religious life, however, was short-lived; regression in many areas and then disappearance in almost all areas quickly followed. In the first half of the eighth century Anglo-Saxon religious women were carrying on significant work outside their native land as missionaries in Germany, but in England itself there may have been trouble brewing; the

Second Council of Clovesho (747) dealt harshly with abuses found in monasteries there. New foundations dropped dramatically, from thirty-eight in the second half of the seventh century to seven in the first half of the eighth century.[1] Whether this was the beginning of monasticism's self-destruction or merely a normal institutional fluctuation cannot be ascertained because by the end of the eighth century outside forces decided the matter. The Viking invasion of England ushered in a period of social and political collapse that witnessed the virtual end not only of expansion but even of almost all existing houses; only one new house was founded there in the second half of the eighth century. The Islamic conquest of Spain and the Maygar invasion of central Europe further added to the chaos of the times.

In Italy Benedict's monastery of Monte Cassino continued to spread its influence, and with the help of Lombard dukes, many existing women's communities lost their autonomy as they were placed under the control and protection of Benedictine monks. Greek communities flourished briefly in Rome when Byzantine women religious fled to the Western monasteries during the Arab and Persian invasions of the Eastern Empire in the seventh and early eighth centuries, but most of these communities were converted into male monasteries by the early ninth century. Little is known about the eighth- and ninth-century Irish communities.

Before the invasions and the ensuing social and political dislocation disrupted religious life in Frankish territory, the Carolingians (successors to the Merovingians) themselves did much to weaken the position of women in monasticism, so much so that it may be wondered whether the invasions and collapse of government actually were beneficial to women religious: It gave them the opportunity to start over again. When the Carolingians emphasized the importance of the private roles for women in society and extended legal rights to women in the domestic sphere, they also limited the public roles of women — and female monastic communities had had very public roles in Merovingian society. With newly extended legal rights in married life and fewer in religious life, being a nun lost some of its attraction. The movement to enforce strict active enclosure (the religious may not leave the monastery) and passive enclosure (no one may enter the monastery) probably did not help in this regard.

As discussed earlier, more than a dozen legislative acts from the period address the issue of enclosure. Enclosure led to many positive results, but the movement to enforce it so strictly at this particular time resulted in the loss of influence and respect for religious women. Rigorous interpretation of enclosure meant women could no longer maintain their schools. Gone was the possibility of a monastery like Whitby graduating five future bishops, or of an abbess like Ita becoming the foster mother of her society's most beloved saints: Women religious deprived of their schools lost an opportunity to mold the next generation. Enclosure also meant their social services to the poor and the pilgrims were curtailed or even eliminated because women religious could no longer maintain hospices within their monasteries. As contact with the outside world was restricted, women's influence in society diminished. In the Merovingian era abbesses did not hesitate to chide bishops or abbots to reform their male monasteries; in the Carolingian era abbesses did not even attend reforming synods. Religious houses slowly became populated by the sick, the disobedient, the unprotected, and the old. The idea of a vocation as necessary for entering a monastery was replaced by the demand of a fee (dowry) to enter.

While all this led to a loss of stature, the changes alone would not account for the extensive damage done to women's religious life had not other changes followed. First, monasteries were increasingly pressured to adopt the *Rule of St. Benedict* in the interest of reform. In many respects women's monasteries benefited by adoption of the rule, but it did place them more firmly under the control of the local bishop and lessen the autonomy of the abbess. Second, the Carolingians initiated a new policy toward monasteries in general. In an effort to consolidate and unify their territory, the Carolingians attempted to make all monasteries, male and female, into royal abbeys. This meant that women's monasteries were controlled from outside their houses by clergy and rulers who did not always grasp the complexities of their life. Monastic reform was a key government policy and culminated in the legislative acts of the reign Louis the Pious (814-840). Veiled virgins and widows with private vows had to join communities, small communities had to merge into one large community, and all communities had to submit to either the *Rule of St. Benedict* or the *Institutio sanctimonialium,* a rule for canonesses compiled by the Council of Chalon in 813 and further refined by the Council of Aix in 816. Women's communities became subject to the whims of secular and ecclesiastical leaders, and as the women had lost an influential voice in society, they had very little recourse to remedy their situation.

They did not have to worry about these matters for long. The collapse of the Carolingian empire and the Scandinavian invasions put an end to strict enclosure, to the loss of influence, to the exploitation of the monasteries — and to the monasteries themselves. In central France only twenty ancient houses survived the Carolingian era, and most other areas in

Europe fared much worse. All may have been destroyed in England, which was still being invaded as late as the eleventh century; in 980 St. Michael's Monastery in Thanet was plundered, and in 1011 the Danes returned to the same monastery and took the abbess hostage. [2]

THE BEGINNING OF THE REVIVAL

Even in this dark, destructive period there were rays of light leading the way to the reestablishment of a vibrant monasticism. The Monastery of Winchcombe for women was founded in England in 787 and a male monastery attached to it in 798. The most prominent medieval Italian women's monastery, the Monastery of St. Salvatore (later called St. Guila) was founded in the mid-eighth century. Numerous foundations for canonesses were made in Germany, ushering in their most prosperous period in that country. The monasteries of Herford and Gandersheim, German centers for female education and culture, were established and grew in prestige during this bleak period. By the latter part of the ninth century female religious life was posed for a revival at least in England, France and Germany.

England

In England Alfred the Great's reign (871-899) heralded a new era for that country. For the next century women, particularly aristocratic women and widows, played a major role in the revitalization of both male and female monasticism. Anglo-Saxon queenship was a high-profile position with much prestige, and from Alfred the Great to King Edgar and the second wave of Danish invasions, most queens were extraordinary monastic supporters and benefactors. Queen Elswitha, Alfred's wife, had Nunnaminster, a women's monastery, built on her property in Winchester. Queen Aelfleda, first wife of Edward the Elder (889-924), was the chief benefactor of England's most important monastic reformer, Dunstan (910-988), and she retired to Nunnaminster after her marriage to Edward was dissolved. His second wife was Edgiva (ca. 902-?), one of the most powerful queens of the era, not only during her husband's reign but also during that of her two sons and even her great-grandson. Perhaps the era's staunchest supporter of monasticism, she assumed her predecessor Aelfleda's patronage of Dunstan and then extended it. By the time Queen Ethelthryth, second wife of Edgar (959-975), came to the throne, the climate was set for all concerned to accept her as the realm's designated "protectress and fearless guardian of the communities of nuns."[3] In the 980s she founded two women's monasteries and heavily endowed them.

Queens were not the only women actively supporting the monastic revival. Many charters, wills, and documents reveal that otherwise unknown women donated estates to women's monastic communities. And women religious themselves were active in the revival. Abbesses participated in the meeting at Winchester ca. 972 that established uniformity throughout all English communities when it issued *The Monastic Agreement of the English Nation for Monks and Nuns*. We know that nuns were present at the conference that preceded and prepared the way for the promulgation of that concordance, that choirs of nuns and monks sang vespers together for the king at the meeting, that abbesses and nuns were invited to assist at the king's coronation in 973, and that they attended a *convivia* given by the queen. Royal, common, religious, and lay women all participated in a monastic revival whose end result was the stabilization and unification of an Anglo-Saxon kingdom and the return of a highly respected life for women.

France

Revival was a bit more complicated in Frankish territory because monastic restriction was the result of many factors besides the invasions. As the strength of the Carolingians waned and then disappeared, so too did many of their policies toward women's monasteries. Ninth-century enclosure turned out to be a policy too early for its time. It returned full force in a few centuries, but for the time being enclosure was rarely enforced. As the power of the king and then the bishop over the monasteries diminished, it fell once more upon the women in the communities to provide the necessary leadership. Women's monasteries became attractive to the upper classes once more. Because of the hard economic times of the ninth century, abbesses actually developed new attributes. While many communities were small, housing perhaps twenty members, others were large enterprises that demanded an abbess with good organizational skills, a keen head for business, and a knowledge of manual labor and agricultural production. The Monastery of Notre Dame de Soissons in 858 housed 216 women religious, 130 male workers, and seventy female workers. It possessed farm land that annually produced three hundred barrels of corn, 350 of vegetables, 2600 of wine, ten of honey, two hundred of salt, and one hundred of tallow for candles.[4] The management of such a business was no easy task. Consequently abbesses who managed such estates were powerful political figures as well, and they played a significant role in both the political developments of feudalism and in the agricultural revolution in the late ninth and tenth centuries.

In the ninth century many women's houses chose to become institutes of canonesses, but by the tenth century it was apparent that although the obligations and functions of Benedictine nuns and of the canonesses were similar, there were more advantages to living under the Benedictine Rule. It was a strict life, but it had the potential of rendering a community more respected, thanks to the rule's strictness and to a Benedictine revival started at Cluny in 909. Women did not directly participate in the Cluniac movement during its first century, but they did benefit from the esteem given to all things Benedictine. Radegund's ancient foundation at Poitiers, Holy Cross monastery, had by then adopted the *Rule of St. Benedict,* and in the tenth century it became the center of a small monastic revival of its own. Three foundations by women for women were made from Holy Cross in the 960s: Trinity, St. Pierre-le-Puellier, and Bonneval-les-Thouras.

Germany

To speak of the revival of women's religious communities in ninth- and tenth-century Germany is not entirely accurate for two reasons. First, women's monasteries had been established only in the eighth century, so they were still developing rather than showing signs of deterioration, and, second, in many areas of Germany invaders had not destroyed the native monasteries. Areas such as Saxony actually witnessed uninterrupted growth of women's religious communities from the eighth through the tenth century. Still, Germany shared in the monastic achievements of the day with the establishment of four exceptional women's monasteries in the north: Herford, Gandersheim, Essem, and Quedlinburg. They all attained exceptional cultural heights and remained the backbone of women's monasticism in the area up until the early modern period.

Although there were two monasteries established in Eastphalia that we know little about, the earliest monastery we have definite facts about is Herford. Herford was founded originally as a dependency of the men's monastery at Corvei, and the men's and women's monasteries together enjoyed immense economic prosperity. Tetta from the monastery in Soissons came to Herford as abbess ca. 838. Gandersheim was founded in 852 and from its beginning was associated with women of Saxon nobility, as were Essen and Quedlinburg. The four monasteries were noted centers of learning. Young girls went to them to be trained in the writings of the patristic and classical eras; some even studied law. The women in these monasteries were extraordinarily talented in the arts as well. (The arts had been emphasized in women's communities since their origin.) We know of at least one instance where women engaged in the production of art. A ninth-century biographer of two Flemish sisters, Harlinde and Renilde, tells us that they were trained in every facet of domestic art as well as in writing, reading, and music, and that they produced beautiful ornate vestments and illuminated jeweled manuscripts.[5] Extant tapestry and embroidery from Saxon monasteries reveal how actively involved these women were in both the arts and the intellectual life; a tenth-century gold embroidered vestment by one Hedwig portrays Martianus Capella's (fl.5th century) story of "The Marriage of Philology to Mercury." The women also were art collectors. Some of the most impressive art of the period was stored in these monasteries.

The real treasure of these monasteries came from Gandersheim in the person of Hrotsvith (932-1000). Founded in 852, Gandersheim's first abbess, Hathumod, had a deep respect for the ascetic life. She insisted that a strict atmosphere pervade the monastery.

> They shared everything; their clothes were alike, neither too rich nor too poor nor made entirely of wool. The sisters were not allowed to dine out with relatives and friends, or to converse with them without leave. They were not allowed like other nuns to leave the monastery to stay with relatives or visit dependent estates. And they were forbidden to eat except at the common table at the appointed times except in case of sickness. At the same hour and in the same place they partook of the same kind of food. They slept together and came together to celebrate the canonical hours. And they set to work together whenever work had to be done.[6]

The monastery also fostered the intellectual life; Hathumod herself had "a stronger power of understanding in listening to or in expounding the scriptures" than any contemporary, her biographer tells us.[7] Discipline and a love of the intellectual life remained the mainstay of the monastery during the next two abbacies of Gerburg (874-897) and Christine (897-919) and resulted in Gandersheim becoming the cultural center of ninth-century Saxony. It comes as no surprise, then, that during the tenth century Gandersheim should be the home and nurturer of Hrotsvith, perhaps the grandest surprise in the cultural history of the Early Middle Ages. How, in a century that produced at best a half-dozen literary writers, did a woman religious become the first dramatist since the classical times and the earliest known poet in Germany?

Hrotsvith's writings show evidence of her knowledge of works of classical writers Terence, Virgil, Lucan Horace, and Ovid and of Christians Prudentius, Sedulius, Fortunatus, Martianus Capella, and Boethius. Obviously Gandersheim's library had depth and breadth. Taking full advantage of the education she received and the sources she was exposed to at Gandersheim, Hrotsvith wrote six dramas in rhymed prose, eight poetic sacred legends, two epics, three long prose prefaces, and numerous letters and shorter pieces. Her historical vision raised her above her immediate time and place: The first third of *Pelagius*, a poetic legend, retells the history of the Saracen conquest of Cordoba; one of her epics relates the history of the early years of Gandersheim; and the other epic deals with the history of a Holy Roman emperor, Otto the Great (962- 973). She preferred classical drama "because of the charm of finished diction"; she disagreed with the denigrating opinion of women classical writers expressed in their works, so she took Terence's "style as a model" and wrote her own drama about holy maidens to correct ancient misogynist presentations. And she did it with boldness. She knowingly invited criticism "because the nature of the work obliged me to concentrate my attention on and apply my mind to the wicked passion of illicit love and to the tempting talk of the amorous," but if she let disapproval of her method and material deter her then "I could not have carried out my purpose." Hrotsvith was a determined woman, intent on accomplishing her self-appointed tasks to the best of her ability. Moreover, she was not dependent on the approval of others: "If anyone is pleased with my work I shall rejoice, but if on account of my unpolished language it pleases no one, what I have done yet remains a satisfaction to myself."[8]

THE REVIVAL IN EARNEST

Cluny

Such an assertive and self-confident statement as Hrotsvith's is rare in tenth-century sources—male or female—but changes in Western society make similar statements almost commonplace by the end of the eleventh century. The agricultural revolution, the growth in population and towns, technical advances, the establishment of strong local authority, and the end of invasions helped the people of Western Europe achieve a new cultural cohesiveness during the hundred years following Hrotsvith's death. Not the least of those factors contributing to this medieval synthesis were the men and women living the ascetic life. During the next three centuries, the High Middle Ages, the religious institutions these people formed and the culture and ideas they incubated therein made an indelible mark on Western culture.

The foundation of the Burgundian monastery of Cluny in 909 marked the beginning of monasticism's new role in the West. Freed from local control, aligned with a papacy that by the mid-eleventh century would itself be transformed into an independent, vital institution, subject to the Benedictine Rule and dedicated to the celebration of the liturgy, Cluny was ideally situated to lead the West into the High Middle Ages. Cluniac monasteries spread rather quickly through neighboring territory, and together with other reform Benedictine monasteries such as Gorze to the north, Brogne in Belgium, Hirsau in Germany, Fruttuari in Italy, and Lexat and Cuixa in Spain, it instilled in society an attraction for strict monastic observance. When women were included in the movement during its second century, it was on much different terms than women religious were accustomed to historically. In 1055, at the height of Cluniac respect, the revered Abbot Hugh (1049-1109) founded a women's monastery at Marcigny, about ten kilometers from Cluny. It was very much a male enterprise from the start, and it had no independent life of its own legally, economically, or spiritually. It was Cluny's property and was ruled directly by the abbot of Cluny himself. Even donations made to Marcigny were recorded as gifts to Cluny and Marcigny.

When the list of inhabitants of the monastery is examined it is apparent that Marcigny was founded to house the female relatives of Cluniac members; Hugh's mother, sisters, and nieces were all members of the Marcigny community, and his male relatives were priors there. Monks were the temporal agents for Marcigny in all transactions, even signing their charters for them. In short, all positions of authority were centered outside of the community of women, a situation unique at this point in the history of women's religious communities.

From another perspective one could look at Marcigny and proclaim that the women there had been given an unprecedented privilege: They had been allowed to join the most respected male community of the day. Marcigny was so completely run by the Cluniac monks that it is difficult to argue that its women were not full members of the Cluniac community. They made their profession to the abbot of Cluny, probably at Cluny, and their customary (the book that detailed the customs, obligations, and traditions of a monastery) indicates they were treated in identical manner as the men. Cluniac spirituality placed great emphasis on the Last Judgment and hence on prayers for the dead; the women at Marcigny shared in the community's remembrances and vice versa. A necrology (a register of the community's dead) written at Marcigny contains a heading "monks of our community."[9]

Cluny founded two other monasteries for women during Hugh's tenure, both in Italy, one near Milan and one near Como. Some priories were founded in the vicinity of Marcigny. There may have been a monastery in Huy, Belgium, and one in Zamora, Spain. None of these appears to be influential. The importance of Marcigny, minimal though it be, rests more on the admiration society had for its disciplined life than on any concrete accomplishment. The women who lived in community (some women were allowed to live as hermits, as were Cluniac men) endured the same rigorous life as the men, and it was a life notorious for its liturgical demands. They also submitted to total enclosure at a time when women's enclosure was not common. One famed story about the monastery concerned a fire near the monastery. As the flames began to threaten the building, neighbors shouted to the women to run for safety. They refused, even after the neighbors' pleas were joined with those of a papal legate who happened to be in the area. The prioress shouted to the crowd from within that rather than waste time trying to get the women out, they should try to put the fire out. Only Abbot Hugh could free them to leave the monastery, fire or not.[10] Such stories epitomized the dedication to religious life and the seriousness with which the women lived that life. Macigny retained society's respect for many generations. When a group of monks broke from Cluny to form the Cistercians in the late eleventh century, they did it specifically to reform the men's monastic life. When that same group eventually established a women's monastery, reform was not their goal. Macigny was in a pure enough state that they instead used it as their model.

Hermits

As the previous discussion indicates, the Cluniac reform did not have a direct or great impact on women's religious life. The reform was, however, the first component of a societal-wide reform movement that gradually affected everyone. The second phase of the movement came in the eleventh century, and at this time women's religious life was very much affected.

The movement started slowly in Italy as a search for the *vita apostolica*, the apostolic life. Such hermits as Romuald and Peter Damian lived and promoted a life based on the principles that had guided the first apostolic community. Particular emphasis was placed on poverty. In this stage the movement manifested itself chiefly in a search for an ascetic, solitary life of poverty. Southern Italy had been the home of a number of Byzantine monasteries throughout the Early Middle Ages, especially after the 730 Iconoclast Controversy in the Byzantine Empire forced many monks and nuns to flee westward, and by the millennium those finding their way to the West were of a decidedly contemplative bend.[11] We know of a hermit named Simon who left Jerusalem to live as a recluse on the estates of Richard St. Vanne in the first decade of the eleventh century, and the Council of Limoges in 1031 noted that there was a settlement of hermits from Mt. Sinai in their territory. Many Byzantine hermits settled in Calabria. These hermits all stirred interest in the eremitic life in the West. Increased access to the writings of the early church fathers and the rise of flamboyant preachers of the ascetic life, first in Italy and then throughout the West, were also major factors.

Women were not strangers to the eremitic life. Female hermits were known to exist throughout the whole of medieval society, and some made deep impressions. We know of eight female hermits honored as saints in England between the sixth and ninth centuries, and twelve in Ireland for about the same period.[12] In the sixth century Italy was the home of six well known hermits, one of whom was the mother of Gregory the Great. Some founders of Merovingian monasteries were either hermits who had communities grow up around them or became hermits after their communities were well established.[13] The total number of hermits is obviously quite low, but they made a significant impact on their society. A few sources allow us to infer that hermits were more numerous than the individual references cite. In Spain, for example, the church thought there were too many hermits in the area, so in the seventh century the Council of Toledo issued mandates regulating their lives.

With the coming of the religious reform movement of the eleventh century, the number of hermits increased dramatically. This produced the paradoxical situation when those wishing to live the solitary life ended up banding together in semi-eremitic communities, a life that tried to combine elements of the eremitic and cenobitic life. The movement involved droves of men and women, rich and poor, who left the urban areas for a solitary ascetic life in forests, caves, and empty spaces. Hermits were especially numerous in Italy and France. Given the nature of life and the duration of the movement, little documentation indicates the exact extent (numbers, places, etcetera) women were involved. As the initial eremitic movement mutated, however, and entered yet another more communal and organized phase, women were found in the first communities that developed from these groups, a fact that indicates their presence all along.[14] In France numerous developments reinforce this conclusion. In 1100 Robert of Arbrissel established a house for women belonging to the group that followed him. Vitalis of Mortain first built a shelter for women hermits in 1105 at Prise-aux-Nonnes; in 1120 it was upgraded and moved to the Monastery of the Trinity at Neufbourg. Salomon built a monastery for these wandering hermits at Noiyseau in 1109, while Alleaume built a monastery for men and women in 1109.

The little we know about hermits before communities were formed is found in sources focusing on other matters or people. We know that the eremitic groups in France were so well known and respected that their reputation spread to England and drew women across the channel to join them; this is revealed in a letter from Goscelin to Eve of Wilton after she so traveled to Angers. In the vita of Godric of Fincale we are told in passing about Godric's sister Burchwine's life as a hermit. William of Malmesbury mentions in the vita of St. Wulstan a relationship one Dunstan had with a woman hermit living near Brumeton. John of Ford's vita of Wulfric of Haselbury includes a tale about Matilda of Wareham's decision to become a hermit. Anselm of Bec names six women hermits in his writings.[15]

The spirited vita of Christina of Markyate offers us a few more details on women hermits, but even here the focus is elsewhere, on her struggles and triumphs rather than on her years as a hermit. It does, however, afford us with a glimpse of how important the presence of such an alternative was in the lives of some women and of the central role women played in the eremitic movement. Christina (1097-1160) was born in the last years of the movement. When still a child she made a private vow of virginity and a decision to become a nun. This caused immediate obvious problems when her parents told her of her arranged betrothal to one Burthred. When she refused to marry him, the drama began in earnest. In a most revealing and exciting narrative the author of the vita proceeds to tell us about all the trials and tribulations Christina had to endure on the way to attaining her goal of being a nun: a forced marriage ceremony; her fight, physical and psychological, not to have the marriage consummated; her mother's out-rageous attempt to find "some way of deflowering" Christina;[16] and her parents' pressure via beatings and humiliations to have her obey. Christina finally escaped her parents' home and rode thirty miles on horseback in six hours to a hermit named Alfwen who, at the risk of her own life, hid Christina from her family. After two years with Alfwen, Christina then secretly moved in with another hermit called Roger and his five male companions in their hermitage. Here she lived confined in a space "not bigger than a span and a half"[17] (13.5 inches) for years so as not to be discovered by her relatives. When Roger died he left Christina the hermitage, which she was not able to inhabit until her marriage was annulled some two years later. When the vita once again speaks of Christina living at the hermitage, it was with other women. During the ensuing years Christina and her group were transformed into a community complete with a monastic complex and church.

Throughout the vita, hermits, both male and female, loom rather largely. Alfwen, Roger, and his five hermit companions were there in the vicinity when Christina needed them. They were willing to help her even though this went against parental authority. They must have enjoyed society's respect or else Christina would not have placed her life nor her reputation in their hands. It is likewise noteworthy that while living such a secluded, secretive life Christina attracted other women from the neighborhood to share the eremitic life with her. Hermits do not appear to be scarce in this time and place. They lived a life of chastity, prayer, and abstinence. When Christina's husband finally released her from her marriage vow various witnesses of comparable social standing were needed for the release to be legal; Roger and his five companions' signatures were recognized as equal to those of Burthred's and Christina's family. Thus, hermits had a recognized authority and role in society.

Anchorites

Hermits—those individuals who lived as the spirit moved them, in solitude, without rules or formal associations with institutions—are rarely found after the mid-twelfth century. Those inclined toward solitude still had options; they could join institutions that fostered the eremitic life, or they could become anchorites, sometimes called recluses. The distinction between a hermit and an anchorite is fine but useful. The *Rule of St. Benedict* uses the terms interchangeably—"Then, the second kind of monks are the anchorites, that is the hermits"[18]—but by the end of the twelfth century the term anchorite was limited to someone living as a hermit in an enclosed abode for life. While references to women hermits disappear in the sources by mid-twelfth century, anchorite literature is relatively abundant. The most well known of this genre is *Ancrene Wisse*, an informal rule or guide for women anchorites of the highest literary quality. Discussions of anchorites are abundant. Most often these women lived in small huts attached to a monastery or a parish church and took a vow never to leave. A formal enclosure ceremony permanently walling up the women inside with no doors and one small window for passing food usually marked the beginning of an anchorite's life. The rigidity of a life so described has to be tempered with the picture we find in such sources as Aelred of Rievaulx's rule for his anchorite sister. In his effort to depict proper behavior for the recluse, he makes his point by comparing it to current improper behavior. "How seldom nowadays will you find a recluse alone. At her window will be seated some garrulous old gossip pouring idle tales into her ears. . . . When darkness falls she welcomes women of even less repute." Before long Aelred has the recluse making the opening to the cell so wide that "what was a cell has now become a brothel." He claims that "evidence abounds that misfortunes of this kind are only too common today among both men and women." His conclusion is succinct: "None of this is for you."[19]

Aelred also tells us that "it is not unknown for a recluse to take up teaching and turn her cell into a school," and then he offers a description of such anchorites that fits many a maladjusted schoolmarm throughout the ages: "Swayed by their childish dispositions, she is angry one minute and smiling the next, now threatening, now flattering, kissing one child and smacking another. When she sees one of them crying after being smacked she calls her close, strokes her cheek, puts her arms around her neck and holds her tight." Such behavior brings distraction and temptation, so the correct behavior is evident: "Never allow children access to your cell."[20]

We know from accounts like this what the ideal anchorite life was and that often the ideal was not attained. On balance, though, these women gained the respect of their society. The laity frequently included them in wills, and the life of an anchorite continued to be an option available to women seeking an intense religious life right up to the Reformation period. This is particularly true in England, where the anchorites flourished in the Late Middle Ages.

4

The Fruits of the
Monastic Revival

During the eleventh and twelfth centuries Benedictine monasteries for women were founded in the farthest recesses of the West. Hungary, Bohemia, Dalmatia, and Spain had monasteries by the beginning of the eleventh century, Poland and Portugal by the twelfth century, and Norway, Sweden, and Denmark shortly after 1100. Even Iceland witnessed the establishment of the monastery of Kirkjubaer in 1186. Benedictine monasticism continued to be a dominant institution in women's religious life for centuries to come, but the most dynamic elements were found outside traditional Benedictine monasticism in the new orders of the day.

Many of these new orders claimed to be reestablishing Benedictine monasticism in its pristine form, but in fact they differed greatly in their interpretation of the rule. The result was a diversification of religious life into many distinctive orders. This mirrored the new complexity of society and was the direct result of society's changes. As the West aroused itself with a flurry of activity in almost every field of human endeavor, many identified the need to reflect upon the direction society was taking and began organizing the eremitical life into institutions. These men and women were not those sheltered from societal changes, but those who were best situated to experience the changes firsthand and to ponder the implications. It is not surprising, then, to see that when the rate of societal change slowed the eremitic movement also slowed—but only after the monastic revival entered into yet another phase and left a legacy of institutions that embodied the fruits of their reflections.

NEW ORDERS

Fontevrault

One of the first groups of hermits to institutionalize their reflective activity was a group in northwestern France who looked to Robert of Arbrissel (1060-1116) for direction. After a very full life, first as a student in the new schools of Paris, then as a reformer for Bishop Sylvester, and finally as a teacher at the cathedral school in Anges, Robert abandoned his budding career as an orator for the life of a hermit in the forests of Craon in the mid 1090s. Around 1100 he and the male hermits gathered around him formed a monastery, this time predominantly for women, at Fontevrault.

Fontevrault was unique. The eremitic movement as a whole attracted the lower classes, but Fontevrault intentionally—at first—was a monastery that welcomed society's outcasts. Women of all backgrounds and status were encouraged to participate in a community life with women in positions similar to their own: One part of the monastery housed widows, virgins, and matrons, another housed repentant prostitutes, and another housed the sick. And although Robert of Abrissel was the founder and the monastery lived under a rule that articulated his ideals, desires, and directions, it is clear that that is all he did. He considered himself to be first and foremost an itinerant preacher. He established Fontevrault out of necessity, to find housing where women "could without scandal live and speak scrupulously with men"[1] together in community. Once that was achieved he "went away freely . . . he did not wish nor was he able to assist with works, for he had to preach to many nations."[2] He traveled and preached for the rest of his life, though he did establish priories dependent on Fontevrault in many places along the way.

The administration of Fontevrault and all its dependent priories was entirely in the hands of the abbess who was "to have and maintain the power or ruling the church of Fontevrault and all of the places belonging to that church, and [nuns as well as brother religious] are to obey her. They are to revere her as their spiritual mother, and all of the affairs of the church, spiritual and secular, are to remain in her hands, or be given to whomever she assigns, just as she decides."[3] All members of the church, men included, acknowledged this complete authority of the abbess. Men were in the order solely to minister to the women in spiritual and material matters.

Fontevrault quickly became identified as a women's religious order of renown, even though it was a double monastery. Correspondence was always addressed to the women, and women were specified as the recipients in almost all the charters of donation. With Robert excusing himself from all administrative tasks, with men obediently performing only the tasks assigned them, and with no ties of obedience to the local bishop, it is clear that responsibility for the success of the order lay to a great extent with the women. This obvious conclusion is often ignored by scholars, who tend to emphasize such things as the good job the men did tending to the business of the monastery in the abbess's name. While this is undeniably true, the administration of the order ultimately fell to the abbesses who, during the twelfth and thirteenth centuries, were almost all exceptional leaders. Moreover, it was the women themselves who maintained discipline and guarded against any behavior that might provide society with an excuse to lower its regard for Fontevrault. This is all the more impressive because Fontevrault in its first years was a haven for social outcasts, although it did not remain so for long. Its success attracted attention from the upper class, and soon the order was a favorite among the aristocracy. Eventually it became the burial grounds for the Plantagenet dynasty of England. During both stages of the order's development, however, the women revealed how efficiently and properly they were able to exercise the extraordinary authority they possessed. Fontevrault continued to establish priories throughout the West and to enjoy the highest regard for the remainder of the High Middle Ages.

The Order of the Paraclete

One of the most overlooked orders founded in the twelfth century, the Paraclete, was paradoxically headed by the most well-known woman of the medieval period, Heloise (1100-1163/64). Reasons for the neglect are understandable. First, it was a small order. Second, Heloise's highly dramatic life tends to tempt historians to pass over the undramatic aspects for the more exciting parts. One of the most promising scholars of her day, Heloise was brought up by an uncle named Fulbert, an archdeacon. He hired Abelard, famed philosopher, theologian, and master of the schools of Paris, to tutor Heloise in private. Within several months they were "caught in the act as the poet says happened to Mars and Venus,"[4] and events unfolded quickly from this point onward. Heloise gave birth to a boy, was married against her better judgment, endured the shock of her uncle's castration of her now-husband Abelard, and was summarily commanded by Abelard to take vows in a monastery. Without any pretense of vocation ("It was your command, not love of God, which made me take the veil," she complained to Abelard[5]), and faithful to her love for Abelard, Heloise nevertheless submitted and lived the life of a model nun. For years she lived without contact or communication from Abelard until he wrote his version of these events, *Historia calamitatum*, some twelve years later. A relationship was then renewed, but in a drastically changed form.

Events conspired once again to draw them together, this time not as frustrated lovers but as cofounders of the Order of the Paraclete. In 1129 Heloise and the community at Argenteuil for whom she was prioress were evicted from their monastery under false pretenses. They turned to Abelard for help. He offered them use of his old oratory, the Paraclete. Heloise proceeded to establish a monastery there for women. Aware after fourteen years of living under the (basically male) Benedictine Rule that it could benefit from some changes before it was truly suitable for women, Heloise approached Abelard for his ideas on the matter. In reply Abelard wrote a lengthy treatise with "some regulations to be a kind of Rule for your calling."[6] Heloise took the treatise to heart but did not adopt it in toto as the monastery's rule. It became the backbone of a rule she eventually wrote herself for her order, adding, omitting, and altering Abelard's rule as she thought need be.

The result was significant. Abelard and Heloise's ideas together created an independent, autonomous monastery for women. It had no formal affiliation with any monastery, nor was it a female branch of a male order. It was not a double monastery with male members, but it did want monasteries of men to be close by and to "be joined by a greater mutual affection."[7] The monastery was to be sustained by an abbess with extensive authority which "no one must presume to oppose . . . or even to grumble at."[8] Abelard had some definitive ideas about the choice and character of an abbess. He considered it to be a "pernicious practice" for virgins to rule as abbesses "rather than women who have known men and been the faithful wife of one husband."[9] Nor should "this election [even] be made from the nobility or the powerful in the world."[10] Rather, the abbess must be "above all the rest in her life and learning, and of the age to promise maturity in conduct; by obedience she should be worthy of giving orders" and "not be ashamed to ask and learn from the lettered" if she is ignorant of a matter.[11] With regard to the monks who have dealings with the nuns, "we make it a rule that they shall impose nothing against the will of the abbess but do everything at her bidding."[12] Such an abbess must be of terribly strong character, able to endure and persevere in her principles in the face of trials and tribulations, even male pressure. In other words, Abelard's ideal abbess was Heloise.

But such an abbess would not just adopt every aspect of a treatise without first subjecting it to a most thorough scrutiny. And Heloise did not. The Paraclete ultimately bears more of the marks of Heloise than Abelard. Abelard wanted "convents of women always to be subject to monasteries of men" and for "the superior of the monks . . . to preside over the nuns."[13] In the Paraclete's final form Heloise as abbess had the last word in all matters and was subject to no abbot. Abelard wanted to allow only seven administrators of the monastery to conduct business outside; Heloise allowed any woman deemed necessary to attend to public affairs.[14] And it was under Heloise's direction, after Abelard's death, that the Paraclete expanded into a religious order with dependent houses administered by the Paraclete abbess. Six daughter houses were founded during Heloise's reign, no small feat given the time and place. And small though it was, the Paraclete Order was revered by all. Heloise was to a great degree responsible for the attention the Paraclete got. The laity in the region demanded "her presence and her spiritual conversation for their guidance,"[15] and leaders as powerful as Peter the Venerable, Abbot of Cluny, believed she had "surpassed all women in carrying out [her] purpose and have gone further than almost every man."[16]

After Heloise's death, though, the order had to earn its respect on its own merit. It got the respect, but it never quite got the recruits that usually followed. In the decades to come, the Paraclete was overshadowed first by female branches of new male orders and then by the mendicant orders. Its last house was closed during the Reign of Terror in 1793, remaining until its end a small, unnoticed order. Still, in twelfth-century France Heloise and the women of the Paraclete were able to establish self-governing monasteries that were treated as equal to even the best of the male monasteries, and that is surely worthy of historical note.

Prémontré

Prémontré was one of the many short-lived monastic orders for women established during the High Middle Ages. It shared much with the order of Fontevrault. They both drew membership from groups that had grown up around charismatic, eremitic leaders aware of the cultural changes of the High Middle Ages. They both provided a new institutional answer to the "Frauenfrage," the question of what to do with the growing surplus of women. Finally, the original vision institutionalized by both orders was experienced too briefly to make any permanent impact on women's lives. The loss of Prémontré's vision was perhaps the sadder of the two.

The first Premonstratensians were male and female hermits who had settled in the forest near Coucy, France, and looked to Norbert of Xanten (1081-1134) as their leader. Women were dominant in this group, and Norbert made it his special mission to accommodate them as well as men. On December 25, 1121, the group formally adopted the *Rule of St. Augustine*, that same rule that religious in Augustine's own day had ignored but one that was congenial to the ideals and goals of these new groups of the High Middle Ages. It emphasizes the biblical mandate to bear witness to society and the principles that guided the first apostolic community. The new groups saw in Augustine's Rule a way to live the *vita apostolica*.

Norbert and his group lived together in a double monastery called Prémontré, and soon they made numerous foundations throughout northeastern France and Germany. At this stage the group was composed overwhelmingly of women. Herman of Tournai tells us (probably in medieval *exaggeratus*) that the diocese of Laon, where Prémontré was located, had one thousand women living in the Premonstratensian houses and that since "daily we see women, not only farm girls or the poor, but also the most noble and wealthy single women and even girls . . . therefore we believe that today these monastic institutions contain more than ten thousand women."[17]

Like Robert of Arbrissel, though, Norbert of Xanten considered himself primarily an itinerant preacher, and by 1125 Norbert's focus was back on his preaching and missionary work. That year he was elected archbishop of Magdeburg, and before long the community at Prémontré elected another abbot. With the new abbot, Hugh, the monastery's identity changed radically. In 1134, the year of Norbert's death, Hugh promulgated the first formal statutes of the order. These statutes changed it from one involved in apostolic work to one dedicated to a traditional, contemplative life. Women were increasingly confined and limited in their work. The next few years witnessed continued dissatisfaction with double monasteries, and in ca. 1141 the first legislation was passed ordering the suppression. From then until the end of the century a struggle persisted over the place of women in the order, and the details allow us to see how ambiguous society's attitude toward women religious had become.

It is not clear whether the decree of 1141 was binding, nor is it clear whether the decree wanted to separate the sexes or to refuse future female members; documentation is sparse. The decree did state that women's monasteries must be at least two leagues distant from the men's. The distance meant administration of pastoral care—saying mass, hearing confessions, and the like—was now more burdensome to the men. Since the women were not given autonomy, the abbot's rule of the women's monastery was also cumbersome. Male members of the order exerted increased pressure to separate themselves from the women. However, the women found a champion of their cause in the papacy. In 1137 Innocent II issued a bull warning the men that they could not move the women without sufficient resources because much of the order's assets had been donated to the order in the women's name. In 1143 Celestine II repeated this warning, as did Eugenius III in 1147 and Adrian IV in 1154. Individual laity also came to the women's aid with donations of land and charters for the establishment of new monasteries. The women themselves contributed most to the failure to enforce the 1141 statute by their persistence in joining the order and their determination to maintain their affiliation with individual male monasteries. They met with repeated success, but the antinun party also pushed ahead. Some male members were vehemently opposed to the presence of women in the order, and the depth of their misogyny is easily seen in one of the most quoted and infamous statements the debate (or any debate of the period) produced.

> We and our whole community of canons, recognizing that the wickedness of women is greater than all the other wickedness of the world, and that there is no anger like that of women, and that the poison of asps and dragons is more curable and less dangerous to men than the familiarity of women, have unanimously decreed for the safety of our souls, no less than for that of our bodies and goods, that we will on no account receive any more sisters to the increase of our perdition, but will avoid them like poisonous animals. [18]

Such outbursts were thankfully rare, and it is apparent that many male members of the order strongly disagreed with the misogynist party and actively supported the women. There was also a third party that argued that maintenance of women's monasteries as originally structured was a financial burden.

In 1198 Innocent III approved the order's legislation, *Concerning the refusal of sisters in the future*, which forbade the admission of any more women. The legislation was not enforced very effectively. Throughout the thirteenth century many in the order continued to flaunt their disregard for both the 1141 statute against double monasteries and the 1198 statute against the reception of women. We know, for instance, of thirty-two houses founded in the lower Rhine River Valley and in Westphalia alone during the twelfth and thirteenth centuries, only eight of which were predominantly male.[19] We also can assume that many other areas were ignoring the directives, because in 1270 the order thought it necessary to issue its strongest repudiation yet of women, forbidding the acceptance of any more women and expelling all who were then in the order to other communities; this time the directive had more success. It is doubtful, however, whether the extinction of Premonstratensian nuns could have come about unless the women ceased to care. By 1270 there were many new options available to women that more fully captured the spirit of the age, particularly the life of a mendicant (embodied by orders such as the Franciscans and Dominicans) and that of a beguine. Women's attention was drawn away from the Premonstratensian Order to these alternatives.

Gilbertines

Like the Premonstratenian Order, the Gilbertine Order, the only religious order founded in England, also grew out of the eremitic movement. In 1131, when Gilbert of Sempringham's search for male candidates for a monastery he wanted to establish was fruitless, he decided to approach seven women hermits already living in the area. When asked, they were amendable to his experiment, so Gilbert proceeded to house them next to a church he had inherited. They were enclosed and followed a rule demanding "obedience, devotion, reverence and respect for the nuns."[20] Originally their needs were met by poor girls in the neighborhood who passed them the necessities of life through a window, but soon these "serving girls asked that a habit be given them with a life of religion, that they might live as part of the family of Christ in a poor but honorable life."[21] Gilbert agreed to their request and thus was born another component of the order, that of *conversae* (lay sisters).

The Gilbertine creation of a lay sisterhood marks an advancement for women, for it made religious life available on a large scale to a class of women previously overlooked. Religious life was never exclusively an option for the upper class (even in the most elite monasteries exceptions were always known), and the first generation at Fontevrault had encouraged admission of prostitutes, but now, with a lay sisterhood, an order specifically addressed the religious aspirations of the lower class. The lay sisters lived a more strenuous life than the enclosed sisters; they were bound by the same vows of chastity, charity, humility, and obedience, plus renunciation of all property and a promise of perseverance. They also had to show obedience, devotion, reverence, and honor to the nuns at all times. Their diet was extremely sparse and their labor extensive; they cooked, sewed, washed, and brewed ale for the community. But they also shared in the nuns' liturgy whenever possible, were taught on feast days by one of the educated nuns, and were respected members of a highly admired community.[22]

Eventually a lay brotherhood for heavy manual labor was added to the order, and then canons for the administration and clerical needs of the now-double monastery. Each component added—lay sisters, lay brothers, and canons—was formed to assist the nuns, the main focus of the order during Gilbert's lifetime: "Be sure that the nuns have everything necessary administered to them more quickly and more faithfully, and be sure that the nuns' church and other buildings are prepared, made and built with more care, more firmly and more nobly than the men's."[23] In the rule Gilbert wrote for them all, surprisingly, the center of authority never rested with the women. One prior ruled the men's house. He was the acknowledged head of the whole community even though three prioresses were elected by the nuns, and they had extensive authority. These women presided over the nuns' and lay sisters' chapter (the meeting of all members of a monastic community where the business of the community was decided, all faults exposed, and problems resolved), dispensed necessary penances, and cared for the sick. Other women officers also had considerable authority. The precentror (officer responsible for church services and hence all liturgical books) was in charge of all the books, which she kept under lock and key. Any canon who wanted a book had to ask her for it, and then she had to approach the nuns' chapter for consent—a very telling detail when assessing the original role of women in the order. In general, the women had control over the internal affairs of the monastery, while the men controlled the external.

Like so many other orders of this century, the nature of the Gilbertines changed drastically after the first generation. Problems within the Gilbertine Order quickened the process of change. Sometime around 1160 a scandal of monumental proportions erupted in the double monastery of Watton, thus providing critics of such monasteries with even more reason to oppose them: A sexual liaison between a nun and a brother led to a pregnancy, a vicious and perverted castration of the brother by the nuns, and a "miraculous" end of the pregnancy without a birth. A revolt in 1165 by the lay brothers exerted even more pressure on the order to make some changes, especially ones pertaining to the separation of men and women. When Roger succeeded Gilbert as prior ca. 1178, the women's position in the order began a gradual downgrading. By the later years of the twelfth century almost all new foundations were for canons only.

Women continued to join the already existing double monasteries, but by the thirteenth century there is evidence that their situation was no longer satisfactory. Documents from 1238, 1247, and 1268 reveal that in specific instances the women lacked the necessities of life.[24] The Gilbertine Order, important as it was for English women in the twelfth century, particularly for lower-class ones, ceased to have a major impact on women's religious life by the end of the thirteenth century.

Cistercians

The impact that the Cistercians had on women's religious life, on the other hand, is difficult to assess. Contrary to all the orders discussed so far in this period, the Cistercians were not founded primarily for women, nor even with women in mind. The Cistercians were founded as a male order by men influenced by the eremitic movement. They were intent not on creating a new rule to accommodate their goals but on revitalizing the Benedictine Rule. Their interpretation of that rule was unique, so their order was indeed just as new as others with similar claims. Women filled with the religious fervor of the day were as attracted as the men to this fresh approach, and they flocked to Cistercian monasteries. At first the men publically rejected them, but the women persisted in their desire to be Cistercians, and by the end of the twelfth century their persistence greatly contributed to a reversal of the men's attitude toward the women. Still, while many women were known as Cistercian nuns during the twelfth and thirteenth centuries, the name was more often than not unofficially attached to them.

Dissatisfied hermits led by Robert of Molesme who were seeking an acceptable form of religious life were responsible for the foundation in 1098 of Cîteaux in central France, the mother house of the Cistercians. In 1112 Bernard of Clairvaux, arguably the most powerful man of his generation, was received into the order. The influx of men increased dramatically thereafter, and many of the new recruits had wives or daughters who desired an identical opportunity. These circumstances led to the foundation of a women's monastery at Tart in 1125; the then abbot of Cîteaux, Stephen Harding, cosponsored its foundation, along with the ducal family of Burgundy, the cathedral chapter at Langres, and the bishop of Langres, but it was not until 1147 that Tart was formally designated as a Cistercian monastery. By that time Tart had many daughter houses. Women's houses that called themselves Cistercian were founded in Switzerland, Norway, England, and Germany. The year 1147 also saw the Cistercian Order form a union with the smaller congregations of Savigny, Obazine, and Cadoiun. These orders also had grown out of the eremitic movement, and they had established women's houses as well as men's. Cistercian legislation and documents say little about the status of these women after the union, but there is every indication that they adopted the Cistercian way of life.[25]

During the next forty years Cistercian monasteries for women multiplied rapidly. Belgium, Denmark, Italy, Portugal, Spain, and Sweden had female monasteries by 1187, and Austria, Luxembourg, and the Netherlands had them by the end of the century. It is in Spain that some of the most interesting developments for Cistercian women occurred. In 1180 the Monastery of Santa Maria la Real was established at Las Huelgas by the royal family of Castile and Leon. In 1187 a bull placing the monastery under papal protection refers to it as Cistercian. The same year the king, Alfonso VIII, petitioned the annual chapter at Cîteaux to allow all Spanish Cistercian abbesses to attend an annual general chapter at Las Huelgas. From this petition it is evident that many Cistercian houses had been founded after 1180 and that the women were already de facto operating their houses quite independent of Cîteaux. In a letter to the abbess of Las Huelgas, Dona María Sol, the abbot of Cîteaux, William II, granted Las Huelgas permission to hold such chapter meetings, to act as mother house of all Spanish Cistercian houses, to select Cistercian clergy as their chaplains, and to enjoy "full participation in all the benefits of our order."[26] This reply is the first written evidence we have of Cistercian women being officially affiliated with the men, although it is quite possible that other women's monasteries for which we have no documentation were affiliated earlier.

One document that did survive reinforces the conception of Las Huelgas as central to the medieval Cistercian experience for women. In 1191 the general chapter at Cîteaux was asked again by founder Alfonso VIII to put its authority behind Las Huelgas' call for all Spanish abbesses to attend a general chapter there. "If they wish to go, as we have already advised them [in the 1187 letter] we shall be glad; but we cannot oblige them to go,"[27] was the monks' reply. Cistercian men deemed it right and proper that Las Huelgas women had sole authority over themselves, and the men had no desire to negate that authority, even at the king's request.

The authority, both civil and religious, of the women at Las Huelgas was truly a rarity. The monastery held court to decide civil cases and matrimonial disputes arising in the sixty-four towns over which it had jurisdiction. It communicated directly with the Roman curia and received its official papal documents. The abbess's authority was even more extraordinary, reminiscent of that exercised by seventh-century Anglo-Saxon and Merovingian abbesses. She had control over the appointment of confessors and the granting of preaching facilities, and sources indicate that she heard confessions and preached. We do know she and not the local bishop blessed novices at their reception and that she presided over the local synods. Such exercise of clerical rights did not go long unnoticed, and in 1210 Innocent III attempted to put an end to these practices. By that time other elements of Las Huelgas' power were already voided by Alfonso VIII's cession of the monastery to Cîteaux, so there was little resistance to Innocent III's demands. Las Huelgas remained a center of women's religious authority for many a decade, but its actual day in the sun was indeed fleeting.

Meanwhile, in the last days of the twelfth century official Cistercian policy toward women apparently changed, although once again we do not have the specific sources to document the reversal. Tart was holding its own general chapters by the end of the century for eighteen of the Cistercian houses in its vicinity with the abbot of Cîteaux in attendance, but we have no statements noting the full incorporation of any women's houses into the order. Houses for women using Cistercian customs, habits, liturgy, and name were establishing themselves at about the same rate as the male houses, and the sheer number of those claiming to be Cistercian put pressure on the general chapter to change its attitude toward the women. In 1198 the Premonstratensian Order suppressed double monasteries and forbade future acceptance of women into the order. Perhaps these two factors—the large number of women already calling themselves Cistercians and the rejection of women by the new orders that originally were their champions—led Cîteaux to reevaluate its position. Whatever the reason, by 1206 Cîteaux was actively trying to regulate the women's lives. That year the monks forbade the women to educate boys in their monasteries, and in 1213 they insisted that all Cistercian women be enclosed.

The latter dictum had the unfortunate result of increasing tensions between the men and the women. Full enclosure of women meant their total dependence on the men for all their needs and their resentment toward the men for the loss of their independence. By 1242 tension reached fever pitch in many women's monasteries; in northern France the women walked out of a meeting with Cistercian monks who had come to relate the contents of restrictive legislation that Cîteaux had just proclaimed. The protest apparently worked in this instance, for the next general chapter annulled the problematic decree. The tension gradually receded by the mid-thirteenth century. Women turned elsewhere in their pursuit of religious life. Communities willing to accept the discipline of Cîteaux were incorporated into the order, and those that were not had other, newer orders and groups to join.

OTHER OPTIONS

Many hermit bands eventually established religious houses like the select groups just discussed. Many left few or no sources, and we know about them only through passing references in other texts. Some were too small to be influential. Others were influential but not often found in the sources or in modern histories, perhaps because they have no modern descendants with a personal stake in keeping that history alive. The Order of Arrouaise, for example, is rarely discussed. It was a popular order of canons and canonesses that did not survive the Middle Ages (ca.1090-1471). Its history follows a now familiar pattern: foundation by a male hermit, initial acceptance of women, and then within its first century the suppression of women's houses.

The most respected and austere eremitic group of the movement, and still revered today, were the Carthusians. The severity of the order's life acted as a natural limit to the growth of the order, and so the Carthusians have never attracted large numbers. It was intended to be a men's order, but women responded to the call as well. Sometime around 1140 the women in the monastery of Prebayon in Provence applied for permission to adopt the Carthusian Rule, and the Carthusian prior of Montrieux, John d'Espagne, granted it. The women followed the order's book of customs and its liturgical practices, and then mixed them with elements of the *Rule for Nuns* of St. Caesarius.

Another entirely different type of male religious life emerged in these centuries, the military order. The Crusades and monasticism merged in a uniquely medieval way to produce orders of monk-soldiers, such as the Teutonic Knights, the Knights of St. John the Hospitaller, the Calatrava Knights, and the Templars. Almost from the beginning women were associated with these orders. When the Templars wrote their rule in 1128, it was clear women were already included in their numbers. The rule forbade any more admissions of women, but many documents prove they still were admitted thereafter.

The rule of the Teutonic Knights allowed women to join. They wore the same habit as the men, had houses in the same neighborhood, and cared for the sick. While some women members of military orders may have likewise busied themselves with charitable works—none, of course, participated in the fighting—eventually most women reverted to a traditional monastic life of prayer and asceticism. None of the military orders had a large number of women's monasteries, but they were widespread and did offer women an alternative. When all of the new orders were closing their doors to women or trying to stop expansion of women's houses, the military orders welcomed women. Women's houses were dependent on the men's houses economically and spiritually, but the women still had a good degree of autonomy within their own community. The abbesses and prioresses were elected by the women, not appointed by the men, and they were left in peace to govern and grow. They declined and then disappeared as the Crusades declined and then disappeared.

Finally, Benedictine monasticism remained a viable and popular option for women in this period. Indeed, it was from within Benedictine monasticism and not the new orders that two of the brightest women thinkers of the era flourished, Hildegard of Bingen (1098-1179) and Elizabeth of Schönau (1129-1165).

Hildegard was a unique woman in many ways. She was the first acknowledged Western female teacher in the church; she fulfilled the roles of preacher and exorcist, roles usually reserved to men; she was a prophet revered by the leaders of the day: Emperor Frederick Barbarossa, Bernard of Clairvaux, and Popes Eugenius III, Adrian IV, and Alexander III were among her correspondents and admirers; and, last, she was a musician, naturalist, artist, dramatist, philosopher, and author of major stature. She even wrote a treatise on medicine. Born in Bermersheim near Mainz of noble parents, she was enclosed in her aunt Jutta's cell at age eight to live the life of an anchorite. The cell was attached to a men's monastery at Disibodenberg, and there Jutta taught Hildegard the Psalter and the ways of monastic life. Together they attracted many followers. Before long the cell multiplied in size and in organization and became a Benedictine monastery of note. Hildegard was elected its abbess in 1136 upon the death of Jutta. The next time we hear of Hildegard she is dictating the visionary and autobiographical masterpiece *Scivias* to her amanuensis, the monk Volmar. This amazing book, complete with illustrations of visions described in minute detail by Hildegard and then executed under her direction, and her seventy liturgical songs still have the power today to evoke strong reaction. Her thought is rich, idiosyncratic, creative, and eccentric all at the same time. Despite her lack of formal education Hildegard's vast knowledge of classical, secular, and patristic writings is evident in all her numerous works. Perhaps their importance is rivaled only by the importance of her roles as prophet and abbess in her contemporary world. What Heloise was to her French world of scholasticism and new monasticism, Hildegard was to her German world of prophecy and Benedictine monasticism.

Elizabeth of Schönau is compared frequently to Hildegard. They were contemporaries from the Rhineland, correspondents, and friends. Elizabeth was thirty-one years Hildegard's junior, and her mystical theology was heavily influenced by Hildegard. At age twelve Elizabeth entered the double monastery at Schönau and at age thirty-three her visions began. She eventually confided in her brother Ekbert, and in 1155 he entered Schönau and became Elizabeth's amanuensis. From then until her death in 1165 Ekbert recorded three diaries for her, numerous letters, a book of revelations, and her popular *Book of the Ways of the Lord*.

Elizabeth's genius was more limited than Hildegard's, but, on the other hand, she was more popular in the medieval world. There were sound reasons for this preference. Her visions and accounts were less allegorical, less traditional, less systematic than Christianity had produced to date, and their originality caught the imagination of the day. Elizabeth's work marks the beginning of a new type of visionary literature that was developed so extensively by women during the next two centuries.

5

The Appeal of the
Vita Apostolica

Developments during the monastic revival of the eleventh and twelfth centuries were both beneficial and detrimental to women. For a few centuries prior to the eleventh century religious life was synonymous with Benedictine monastic life. By the end of the twelfth century there was a wide variety of different religious orders, only one of which was Benedictine monasticism. Women certainly had numerous options and opportunities as a result. Religious life was more readily available to more classes of women. The multiplication of monasteries was possible because society revered the life enough to support it, and thus more women were the recipients of society's respect. The spread of women's houses into the remote areas of Europe meant that even those women previously denied alternatives to married life now had one. And the overall increase in the number of women belonging to religious communities of course meant that more women were being educated, enjoying an intellectual life, exercising authority, and being viewed as models of behavior by the lay society surrounding them.

Some less favorable conclusions are also evident in the study of the eleventh- and twelfth-century monastic revival. With the exception of the Order of the Paraclete, the foundations, the guiding spirit, and the rules of the new groups were all initiated by men. Women did not contribute to the formation of these groups in any way close to the degree they did in the ages of Melanie the Elder or Brigid of Kildare. Perhaps even more noticeable is the lack of individual visibility that the women involved in the new orders had, again with the exception of Heloise. Some abbesses are identified by name and discussed in the records of the time, but unless one had a highly dramatic life (as did Christina of Markyate) or excelled in areas other than those directly related to religious life (as did Hildegard of Bingen), the sources spend little time on the women in these orders. Male chroniclers writing for male audiences choosing to concentrate on male accomplishments might account for some of the invisibility of women religious leaders during the period, but since this condition holds true for all periods discussed so far, it is hard to argue that this is the reason. All evidence points to the conclusion that while the eleventh and twelfth centuries provided women with more options, female initiative was not fostered or encouraged. Women were very much present in all aspects of the movement and contributed in vital ways to its success, but only rarely were they considered the spiritual authors of the groups or remembered as founders.

In the thirteenth century women once more gained visibility as leaders and innovators in religious life when the medieval monastic revival entered its final phase. In Chapter 4 discussion centered on religious orders formed when various unorganized groups institutionalized their way of life. Not all groups, however, became officially accepted or officially recognized religious orders. We need now to discuss this whole other stratum of groups, which were dominated by an intense desire to live the *vita apostolica* to the fullest, as described in Acts 4:32 and Luke 10:1-12. The groups' identifying characteristics were an emphasis on poverty and on communal living. The women in these groups were called various names: *mulieres sanctae, bizoke,* beguines, *humiliati, papelarda, coquenunnea,* and *pinzochere,* to list a few. Since they often lived on the outskirts of society in the years before a decision of acceptance or condemnation occurred, there was a span of time when groups that later generations would reject as unorthodox were viable options for women seeking a noninstitutionalized form of religious life.

UNORTHODOX GROUPS

Cathars and Waldensians

Two of these unorthodox groups, the Cathars and the Waldensians, eventually were declared heretical, but since women played a major role in each sect in the days prior to their condemnation, they will be discussed here. The Cathars were called Bogomiles in the Balkans when they first appeared in the Early Middle Ages, Cathars when they spread into northern Italy and southern France in the eleventh century, and Albigensians when the town of Albi in Languedoc became their stronghold in the twelfth century. The Cathars' deeply dualistic doctrine was not kind toward women; woman was, according to Eckbert, bishop of Schönau, "the fruit that God had forbade Adam to eat in the garden . . . and therefore the whole human race born of women is born of fornication."[1] But the goal of the Cathars (from the Greek, *katharos*, pure) was to become purified from all matter, and this goal could be attained by women as well as men. The *perfecti* (or *electi*, elect), the perfect who achieved total purification, were venerated by the believers, those still striving for purification. Women *perfecti* could and did enjoy higher status and authority than all men and women believers; only the men *perfecti* were higher. When there were no men *perfecti* present the women *perfecti* led the community in prayer, and their authority could not be challenged. Such women were considered to possess the fullness of the Spirit, and in a sense they enjoyed a more exalted position in the Cathar community than an abbess in the monastic community. Houses of women *perfecti* populated the countryside wherever Catharism flourished, serving as centers for the evangelization the sect engaged in. Many houses also were centers for cottage industries, and young girls often were placed in them for economic reasons. Most inhabitants, though, were true believers who adhered to the rigid discipline of the Cathar house.

In 1173 a man named Valdes (Peter Waldo) from Lyons experienced a classic conversion, similar to the type Francis of Assisi would make so famous in a few years: A merchant struck by the hollowness of life hears the biblical command in Luke 10:1-12 to sell all and follow Jesus radically changes his life to follow the mandate literally. Within six years of Valdes' conversion a large group also intent on fulfilling the command had gathered around him. Women were among the most faithful followers in the group. They found the Waldensians congenial to their desire for an intense religious life. Waldensian doctrine contained no blatant misogynist tenets as did the Catharian; neither did it hold forth an exalted position for women equivalent to the *perfecti*. However, all were obliged to spread the word, which meant that Waldensian women were preachers. Women preachers had to meet the same standards as the men, and training was necessary, sometimes as long as six years. Heavy emphasis was placed on scripture, and schools for the community were maintained in homes to teach scripture. Those not able to read often memorized lengthy sections of the Bible.

It was easy for the church to identify the heretical elements in the Cathar community; it was not easy where the Waldensians were concerned. At the Lateran Council in 1179 the Pope applauded the Waldensians' piety and granted them unofficial approval, yet five years later approval was withdrawn and condemnation was levied. Groups other than the Cathars and Waldensians were sprouting up spontaneously throughout the West, and many walked a thin line between orthodoxy and heterodoxy. Innocent III (1198-1216) saw the potential these groups could have in the church if properly sanitized of heretical tendencies and harnessed for the church's benefit. His dealings with another group, the *Humiliati*, are instructive. In 1199 Innocent III ordered the bishop of Verona to stop classifying all *vita apostolica* groups as heretical without first thoroughly examining their beliefs for orthodoxy. Reports of the excommunication of the *Humiliati* had reached Innocent's ear, and he believed that if this group could be unified under an approved rule they could be an asset to the church. To that end he set up a commission to study the problem, and in 1201 Innocent formally recognized the *Humiliati*. For years after, the group was popularly perceived to be heretical, but in the long run Innocent achieved his goal: The *Humiliati* remained orthodox. The *Humiliati* were active in saving other *vita apostolica* groups from adopting heretical doctrine, and they helped prepare the way for official acceptance of the two most successful orthodox *vita apostolica* groups of the Middle Ages, the Franciscans and the Dominicans.

ORTHODOX GROUPS

The Poor Ladies: Second Order of St. Francis

People who know little else about the Middle Ages usually know of Francis of Assisi (1181/82-1226). His power to attract followers was legendary in his own time, and it has remained so throughout the centuries. At first glance his life and goals differed little from other men and women in the search of the true apostolic life, but there was something unique about Francis, something that defies historical analysis. His personality was apparently one of the most charismatic in the history of the West, judging from the impression he made on his contemporaries. Having noted this, we also must note that the last few decades of research have done much to place Francis' accomplishments in their historical context, and we now see the religious order that formed around him not quite as revolutionary as once thought. The Franciscans were simply the most successful and most popular of these groups with whom they shared so much. Francis' disciples drew the best of all practices, virtues, and ideals from the movement into an institutional form of life that was but the logical culmination of the monastic reform movement begun at Cluny.

The Franciscans' beginning follows a familiar pattern. Francis was born into a wealthy family, and during his youth was busy following in his merchant father's footsteps, until he underwent a dramatic conversion. At first he lived as a hermit in caves and in church ruins, and a few men gathered around him. In 1208 Francis heard a sermon on Matthew 10:7-9, the classic preaching directive given to the first apostles, and he responded on the spot: "This is what I wish; this is what I seek."[2] He removed his sandals and tunic right there and embarked on a life of total poverty and preaching.

Francis and his small group of eleven traveled to Rome in 1209-10 to have Innocent III approve a rule for them. This was the beginning of the Franciscan Order, whose members, along with Dominicans and Carmelites, often are referred to as friars or mendicants. Women became a part of the Franciscan movement two years later when Clare of Assisi (1194-1253) joined the group. When Clare's reputation for sanctity became known to Francis, he arranged to meet her so he could persuade her to place herself under his guidance, and "the virgin delayed not long her consent."[3] She made her profession to Francis and his friars and "laid the foundation of the Order of the Poor Ladies."[4] (In the early sources the Second Order of Franciscans was called the Poor Ladies; within a few generations they were more commonly called the Poor Clares.) She then went to live with some Benedictine nuns first at Bastia and then at Panso, but "she enjoyed no peace of mind there,"[5] because life as a traditional monastic nun was not what she had envisioned when she agreed to make a profession to Francis' community. She wanted and expected to live the same type of life and achieve the same goals as the friars.

The next we know of her she had been joined by her sister Agnes and the two of them were residing at St. Damian's, a church that Francis had restored. Clare then got her wish to live as the friars did, and she and Agnes were joined by many other women. Jacques de Vitry (1160/70-1240), a renowned champion of women religious, in a letter dated 1216, gives us the only lengthy description of the women that we have from the period.

> I was consoled by seeing a great number of men and women who renounced all their possessions and left the world for love of Christ: "brothers minor" and "sisters minor," as they are called. They are held in great esteem by the lord pope and the cardinals. They are detached

completely from temporal things but have one fervent desire to which they devote all their efforts: to convert souls that are in danger from the vanities of the world and to prevail upon them to imitate their example. . . . They live just like the first Christian community, about which it is written: "The multitude of believers were of one heart and one mind." By day they enter the cities and villages, devoting their attention to activities that others profit from, and at night they return to their hermitages or to a solitary, isolated place to contemplate. The women, in fact, live together near the cities in various hospices. They accept no wages but live by the labor of their hands.[6]

It is clear that Jacques de Vitry considered the lives of the men and women to be the same, and he implies that his contemporaries did so too. Both possessed the same characteristics and the same virtues. Clare herself claims that even Francis considered the women's lives to embody the same Franciscan ideals as the men's in her *Testament* and in her *Rule* when discussing the *formula vitae* (form of life) Francis wrote for her group in 1215.[7] She stated that once Francis and his community "saw that although we are physically weak and frail, we did not shrink from deprivation, poverty, hard work, distress or the shame or contempt of the world— rather as he and his brothers often saw for themselves, we considered following the example of the saints to be most satisfactory; he rejoiced greatly in the Lord."[8]

Something happened, though, in late 1215 or early 1216, for Clare must have believed the women's pursuit of Franciscan life was being challenged. She went directly to the pope for aid. Innocent III responded with an extremely important and unique papal bull, the *Privilege of Poverty*, written in his own hand. It was granted to all women "who both at present or in the future make perpetual profession of the [Poor Ladies] regular life" characterized by poverty and imitation of Christ, and warned all interested parties that the Poor Ladies "can be forced by no one to receive possessions." Moreover, "if in the future any ecclesiastical or regular person, knowing about this confirmation shall attempt to act contrary to this confirmation, he is deprived of any position of power and honor . . . and is excluded from the all holy body and blood of God the Lord . . . and in the Last Judgement is liable to severe punishment."[9]

This privilege is a rarity in the history of female religious orders. To date, the Poor Ladies are the only order of women to be so encompassed by papal protection. As such, this privilege marks the high point of not only the Poor Ladies but also of all medieval women in pursuit of the *vita apostolica*. It also, unfortunately, marks the end of one phase of the order and the beginning of another in which its nature was radically changed.

In August 1218, Pope Honorius III (Innocent III having died in 1216) appointed Hugolini Segni as cardinal protector of both male and female Franciscans. Within days of the appointment Hugolini got Honorius III to issue a bull that gave ownership of all Poor Ladies' houses to the papacy, and within months Hugolini imposed a basically Benedictine rule on all the Ladies. The new rule contained significant changes in their spiritual life and in their physical life: The Franciscan concepts of poverty and imitation of Christ, the two defining observances of the women, were ignored, and strict enclosure was demanded. Gone were the days when the Poor Ladies could be described as Jacques de Vitry had, living "just like the first Christian community." We have no record of Clare's reaction specifically to enclosure, but we do know that nine years later she was still fighting for the Poor Ladies' right to observe poverty and imitation of Christ. Hugolini was now Pope Gregory IX, and while attending Francis' canonization in Assisi in 1228 he stopped by Clare's monastery to pressure her to abandon all pretense of poverty and "to consent to some possessions."[10] Her answer was immediate and defiant: "she emphatically opposed it and refused to agree." Her justification was equally to the point: "Never do I wish to be released from following as closely as possible in the footsteps of Jesus Christ."[11] Poverty and imitation of Christ were extricably linked, and she would give up neither.

Instead of transgressing the Poor Ladies' original privilege blatantly and bringing down Innocent III's anathema and call for deposition upon himself, Gregory IX rendered it innocuous by reissuing it two months later minus its key elements: He deleted mention of the applicability of the privilege to future as well as present members, he deleted the original privilege's command that anyone who did not live in poverty must leave the monastery, and he substituted Innocent III's call for excommunication, deposition, and eternal punishment of any transgressor with a mild chastisement that such a person would "encourage the indignation of Almighty God."[12] His policy was clear. Poverty was no longer to be the Poor Ladies' identifying trait. He tolerated its observance in Clare's own monastery only as an exception and only if the other women there agreed to it. The following year he began enforcing his policy. He compelled a Poor Ladies' house a few miles from Clare's to accept possessions, and thereafter he repeated this policy every chance he had.

For the rest of her life Clare valiantly argued for the retention of what she always considered were the Poor Ladies' chief goals, imitation of Christ and poverty. Even though modern historians have tended to see enforced enclosure of the Poor Ladies as the main issue in this tale, Clare did not. Enclosure was not a point of contention with her, for she believed imitation of Christ and poverty could be achieved inside as well as outside a monastery. To give up the Poor Ladies' desire to be true imitators of Christ, however, was unthinkable to her, and so she fought with the papacy literally until her death to retain this right. Hours before she died the papacy finally approved a rule she had written for the Poor Ladies that embodied their original goals. The approval was a token gesture at best, for it was observed only at Clare's and Agnes' houses. Within ten years of Clare's death the papacy imposed on all the remaining 120 Poor Ladies' houses a different rule that forbade the practice of absolute poverty.

Clare was an exceptional woman on many levels, but the story of her order and the hierarchy's attitude toward it was somewhat typical for the period. Clare was an outstanding leader and founder, with the same degree of intelligence, organizational competence, and personal charisma that women like the Melanies of old possessed. Her courage and determination were legendary, and when she believed she was right she persisted until victory, no matter how high an authority stood in her way. When the Pope forbade the friars to preach to the Poor Ladies without his permission, for example, Clare commanded the women to go on a hunger strike until he rescinded his order: "When Pope Gregory heard this, he immediately mitigated his prohibition."[13] She was a theologian in her own right, and few if any thirteenth-century religious thinkers had a more explicit understanding of the obligation of religious to bear witness in their society than she. To Clare the future health of religious order lay in its ability to construct a life that fostered such witness.

> For the Lord himself has set us an example and mirror for others, even for our own sisters whom the Lord has called to our life, in order that they themselves may then become mirrors and examples in the world. The Lord has, therefore, called us to great things, that in us others may see an example and mirror. . . . Because of this if we live according to the following form, we will leave to others a noble example and we will acquire eternal happiness for very little labor.[14]

The clerical response to Clare, with few exceptions (Jacques de Vitry being the most famous) was unenthusiastic and, ultimately, unsupportive. Francis does not appear too admirable in this tale. He recruited her, yet once he realized the complexities of having women active in apostolic work in his order, he became unresponsive to the needs of her order. Most clergy reacted the same way. Even if they were initially supportive of women living the *vita apostolica*, they soon became uncomfortable with the situation. The thirteenth-century society saw increased efforts to channel women religious back into a traditional monastic form of life. To this end a movement to enclose women permanently was born, and as we have already noted, this time it was more successful than in the past. In the last days of the century the papal bull of 1298 *Periculoso* proclaimed "every nun, individually and as a group, present and in the future, of whatever order or congregation, in whatever part of the world they may be, shall from this time forward, remain in the monasteries in perpetual enclosure."[15]

Dominicans

Dominican women were channeled almost right from their beginnings into enclosure, even though the origins of the order were rooted in the desire to live the *vita apostolica*. When faced at the turn of the thirteenth century with the challenge of trying to discourage people in the region of Albi from joining the now-heretical Cathars, Diego de Acerbo and his companions believed the best way to do so was to go among them as orthodox followers of the apostolic life. The approach was a huge success. After Diego's death in 1207, Dominic assumed leadership of the group and decided to institutionalize his followers into a religious order formally known as the Order of Preachers, but most often called the Dominican Order. The first institution he actually founded, however, was not for men but for women. In 1206 he established a monastery at Prouille "to house some noble women." Their activities differed radically from the men: "they keep strict silence and perpetual enclosure; they work with their hands to avoid laziness and idleness."[16] Still many, including the women in the order, saw the work of the sisters as just another facet or expression of the task all Dominicans were dedicated to, giving others witness to the *vita apostolica*: "The excellence of their lives and the purity of their consciences gain salvation for themselves and give an example to others. . . . Both in numbers and in merit they have increased beyond telling, so that the fragrance of their sanctity has spread far and wide, inspiring many devout women to follow their holy example, and establish similar communities elsewhere."[17]

Before long there were Dominican houses for women in Rome, Madrid, and Toulouse. In Bologna one of the most powerful women of the town, Diana Andalo, began to "spend more time in the company of the Friar Preachers" and "when St. Dominic came to Bologna . . . she put herself in his hands." Soon so "many other noble ladies and illustrious women of Bologna followed her example and began to spend time with the Friars Preachers" that Diana made a vow to establish a house for the Dominican women.[18] The chronicle of St. Agnes' Monastery, the house she eventually founded, gives us insight into the role the women played in the order. It tells us Diana "began to discuss with St. Dominic how she could put [the vow] into effect." He "gathered his brethren and asked them what they thought about building a house of nuns which would be called and which would be a part of the Order. The brethren answered as they thought fit," and after a day of prayer Dominic declared, "It is absolutely necessary, brethren, that a house of nuns should be built, even if it means leaving off for a time the work of our own house."[19]

Dominic, it appears, had a strong positive initial response to the presence of women in the order he had established, as did Francis. But unlike Francis, Dominic never conceived of the women in his order as members living the same life as the men. Clare and the first Poor Ladies at first did live similar lives to the men, and when they became problematic, Francis and the hierarchy withdrew their support for the women's original apostolate and gradually pressured them into another form of life. Such a reversal was not necessary in the Dominican Order. Dominic saw two types of life as necessary and complementary to achieve the overall goal of the Order of Preachers, the active life of Martha and the contemplative life of Mary. Dominic and his group were involved in an active apostolate, but before he officially institutionalized it, he established a contemplative base at Prouille for women. Once it was assured that part of the Dominican Order was busy with the work of Mary, Dominic then proceeded to open houses for the men and the work of Martha. We find the same sequence of events in the story of Bologna. Building the men's houses would come after the building of the women's contemplative house. The priority of the Dominicans was clear. The contemplative life was superior, an essential prerequisite and necessary food for the active life.

That women were given the role that was, in the eyes of the Dominicans, superior has been little noted. Modern historians too often look at the active life of the Dominican friar in the town and university, compare it to the enclosed, withdrawn life of the Dominican nun, and conclude that women were given an inferior, invisible, and superficial role. In Dominican theology nothing could be further from the truth, for their theology gave the enclosed nun a new role. The enclosed nun was a partner in the apostolate and the lifeblood of the whole order. Without the presence of the contemplative houses of women, the active houses of men could not thrive. The women's houses gave witness to the *vita apostolica* in every area they were found. The women in the order were not an afterthought, as with the Cistercians, or a burden, as with the Franciscans, but integral, equal partners and pursuers of the life of Martha and Mary.

Only twice during the early years do we know of any Dominicans challenging the position of a women's house in the order, and the challenges were quickly rebuffed. In the face of some criticism, Dominic's successor, "Master Jordan, together with the definitors at the general chapter in Paris, held urgent consultations with some masters of Paris University and their unanimous verdict was that they could not separate the nuns' house from their charge without mortal sin. Then the blessed father severely reprimanded the friars who had complained or raised questions about this house."[20] However, during Raymond of Penafort's rule as minister-general (1238-1240), an antinun party gained increasing influence in chapter legislation. By 1243 the nuns turned to the papal curia for help, and by 1267 the argument over nuns' position within the order was resolved to the women's satisfaction and according to Dominic's original vision.

Enclosure certainly eliminated the possibility of an active life, but there was never any indication that women joined the Dominicans in search of such a life. Women joined because it was clear they could live a contemplative life therein. For those wishing an active life there was an alternative, an experiment of sorts going on in northern Europe, very similar to the heretical groups but in the final analysis orthodox. The movement was never organized into a religious order, but it provided a form of religious life that numerous women found extremely attractive.

Beguines

The history of the beguines does not come to us easily. Movements that eventually organized into religious orders usually have the advantage of having the story of their origin preserved. The beguines never had any particular self-interest in preserving their history, and hence information is gleaned mostly from sources outside the movement itself and most often from a local perspective. Moreover, beguine communities had little if any contact with each other. The piecing together of their history is quite tentative and has not been attempted before our own time.

Another reason that their origins are hard to identify is because the beguines were one of many, many groups that fashioned their lives around the principles of the *vita apostolica* and that were in their first years virtually indistinguishable from each other. Some of these groups that lived in the Low

Countries during the twelfth century eventually became known as beguines. By the beginning of the thirteenth century the women in the diocese of Liège were so identified, and chief among them was the woman many consider the prototype beguine, Mary of Oignies (1177/78-1213). Mary was born in Brabant of wealthy parents, and at the age of fourteen she married a man who soon shared her desire for the apostolic life. Together they vowed to live in chastity and converted their home into a leper hospital. Her reputation for sanctity and mysticism spread far and wide, and many women in the area already pursuing a similar life of lay apostolic work looked to her as a model. The attention she enjoyed led her to seek her husband's permission to withdraw to a cell in Oignies. In the later years of her short life she befriended and inspired many preachers and apostolic workers. With no preacher did she work more closely or influence more deeply than Jacques de Vitry, the beguines' most outspoken advocate. Jacques insisted that he was Mary's deputy and instrument; he was ordained at Mary's request and he preached under her guidance. It is to him that we owe much information about Mary and the first beguines, for in his effort to defend and protect their form of life he wrote Mary's vita.

According to Jacques de Vitry, the beguines offered women in pursuit of the *vita apostolica* an orthodox alternative both to heretical groups and to women's religious orders that mandated enclosure. It was a way of life that gave women the independence of the Cathar *perfecti* and the mobility of the *Humiliati*. The beguines vowed to remain chaste and obedient as long as they lived in a beguinage, a house of the beguines. They placed great emphasis on the redeeming value of manual work and in most instances lived in poverty mitigated by weaving, spinning, carding, sewing, and the education of children. The life, Jacques tells us, was simple, sparse and admirable:

> Under the discipline of one who is superior to others in honesty and prudence, they are instructed in the rule and the literature, in vigils and prayers, in fasts and various afflictions, in manual work and poverty, in self-effacement and humility. For we see many who, scorning the riches of their parents and rejecting the contemptible and wealthy husbands offered them, live in profound poverty, without anything but what they can acquire by spinning and working with their own hands, content with vile clothes and modest food.[21]

Their spirituality anticipated themes that dominate not only women's groups during the Late Middle Ages but eventually all lay piety. They developed a zealous attachment to the sacraments, in particular to the sacrament of the Eucharist and the human presence of Christ therein. Again Jacques de Vitry's description of Mary's love of the Eucharist is revealing, for its vivid physicality became typical in Eucharistic devotions of future generations: "The sacred bread strengthened her heart; the sacred wine intoxicated her, making her spirit overjoyed. The sacred bread filled her and the life-giving blood pulsated throughout her body. It pained her deeply when she abstained very long from receiving it. For Mary, to live was the same as to eat the body of Christ, and this was to die: to abstain too long a time from the sacrament."[22] The popularity of Eucharistic devotion among the beguines continued to increase dramatically in the decades after Mary's death and culminated in the establishment of the feast of Corpus Christi. Juliana of Cornillion (1192-1258) was responsible for the church's official adoption of the feast, but its overwhelmingly positive reception in late medieval village and town life cannot be explained without acknowledging the laity's openness toward women's spiritual leadership. The widespread acceptance of the feast and the popularity of its related devotions is a milestone in the history of Western Christian piety, for women played a more significant role in the establishment of this universally observed feast than in any previous feast.

The first generation or two of beguines were left in relative freedom to develop their own unique form of life, but by 1233 the freedom began to be curtailed. In that year Gregory IX issued the bull *Glorium virginalem*, which offered the informal women's groups Rome's approval. This signaled the end of the beguines being labeled heretics and the beginning of the recognition of the groups' orthodoxy by local bishops. Clerical direction and then control often followed, although it would be wrong to conclude that clerical interference always was negative or so persuasive that it altered the nature of the movement. Beguines remained religious laywomen active in charitable works who commanded respect wherever they settled. They had thriving communities in Italy, parts of central Europe, and southern France. Their influence was immense during this stage of their history, especially on spirituality. The mystical movement and the *devotio moderna*, two related movements of spirituality and piety that swept over Germany during the late medieval period, had some of their roots in beguine spirituality; the mystical writings of the beguine Hadewijh were known in the houses of the Canons Regular of Windesheim, the eminent center for the *devotio moderna*. By the fifteenth century, however, the first phase of the movement was spent, and the beguinages that remained resembled more closely shelters for working-class poor than houses of religious women. The beguines experienced a remarkable revival in the seventeenth century and survived into the twentieth.

Still, the significance of the beguines should be emphasized. In their immediate world the beguines offered women an orthodox equivalent to heretical *vita apostolica* groups. Second, they were groups that women themselves directed. They were outside the bounds of monastic control and, originally, of diocesan control; beguines were independent women. Third, some beguines were powerful beyond their own circle of women. Mary of Oignies, for example, was the supporter and director of many a cleric and a voice of authority among the laity. Fourth, they offered women a type of religious life that was adaptable to the new urban environment of the day. In southern Europe the male mendicants met this need, but it was female beguines who supplied the solution in the north. Last, the beguine movement was at its birth and remained until its final days a *via media*, a life for women somewhere between that of a nun and a laywoman. Future generations often used the beguine movement as a model when they set out to create their own variation of religious life.

Helfta

The effect beguine spirituality had on all Western Christian spirituality already has been alluded to, but in one women's monastery beguine spirituality combined with other major spiritualities of the period to produce a center of women's spiritual leadership unequaled since the days of Hrotsvith's Gandersheim. In 1229 Burchard and Elizabeth of Mansfield founded what they thought would be a Cistercian monastery for some women from Halberstadt. The house was never acknowledged by the Cistercians, although the women did observe many Cistercian practices. The group expanded enough to force a move to Rodarsdorf in 1234 for larger quarters, and then again in 1258 to Helfta for the same reason. The first abbess was Cuengunde von Halberstaat, but with the election of Gertrude of Hackeborn (1232-1291) as abbess in 1251, Helfta began a fifty-year period of spiritual prosperity that made an indelible mark on Western spirituality. Sometime during Gertrude of Hackeborn's reign Helfta began using Dominican confessors, thus introducing Dominican spirituality into the monastery. In 1270 Mechthild of Magdeburg (1210?-1294?) joined the group and brought with her a third spiritual strain, beguine. Mechthild became a beguine when she was twenty-two or twenty-three, and later a Dominican tertiary (member of a "third order"; the first order of a religious order was for clerics, the second for nuns, and the third for laity, male and female). She was vocal enough in her criticism of church abuses that she sought protection from her detractors among the revered women of Helfta. Mechtild's presence there and the combination of Cistercian, Dominican, and beguine spiritualities acted as yeast, and in the last two decades of the century Helfta produced three authors and three masterpieces of mysticism.

Gertrude of Hackeborn was not herself a writer, but her insistence that the women in her monastery pursue the study of liberal arts as well as scripture is largely responsible for the atmosphere Mechthild of Madgeburg found when she arrived. Two women were already flourishing spiritually at Helfta when Mechthild of Madgeburg arrived: Mechthild of Hackeborn (1240-1298?), the abbess Gertrude of Hackeborn's younger natural sister; and Gertrude the Great (1256-1302?), sometimes called Gertrude of Helfta. Indeed, Mechthild of Madgeburg went to Helfta in the belief that "God might direct her to someone there who could assist her spiritually." She was not disappointed. When "the beguine had a conversation with St. Mechthild, sister of the abbess, [she] was enchanted by her" and then was told by God, "I am working great things in Mechthild but those which I am working and shall work in Gertrude are much greater."[23] Mechthild of Madgeburg's reputation preceded her; she had already written all but the seventh (and last) part of her masterpiece *The Flowing Light of the Divinity*, and the Helfta women were aware of it. It was written in prose and poetry and in Low German rather than in Latin, thereby making the text more accessible to a larger audience and exposing more people to mystical spirituality. Mechthild of Madgeburg is one of the first medieval writers to use the vernacular. It was the spiritual rather than the literary content, however, that had such an effect of Helfta. Before long the two other Helfta masterpieces were produced, Mechthild of Hackeborn's *Book of Special Graces* (1291) and Gertrude the Great's *The Herald of Divine Love* (1289).

With these women of Helfta we have the beginning of a new phenomenon in Western Christianity, the powerful woman mystic. These women did not depend on outside clerical direction or ecclesiastical office as the basis of their own authority, although that is not to imply they were disrespectful of the clergy. They simply bypassed hierarchical direction and anchored their authority in the will of God as revealed to them, as do mystics by definition. As such, their authority extended beyond the monastery's walls and, when appropriate, over clerical heads. During the next two centuries some women exercised unusual authority in certain situations that would be inexplicable if one was not aware of the transcendent power mysticism imposes on the mystic; Catherine of Siena's (1347-1380) central role in resolving the problems that plagued the Avignon papacy of her day is the most obvious of many possible examples. Mysticism transcends gender; thus these women were not seen as women appropriating male roles but as mediators, and preachers, and teachers of God's own choosing. The women of Helfta stand at the beginning of a new tradition, one that can be seen as a viable substitute for the fading tradition of the powerful abbess.

Other Orthodox Groups

It has been noted throughout that this is a selective rather than comprehensive survey of women's religious life. This holds true tenfold for this chapter and all subsequent ones, for the options available to women multiply dramatically from the late medieval period into the modern era. The history of women's religious life in the matter of diversification correlates to the history of society in general. As Western society became more and more complex, the forms of religious life created to respond to the needs of a complex world multiplied as rapidly.

Sometimes we become more aware of the vast variety of religious forms of life or of a new apostolate by chance mention in sources dealing with other topics. We know, for example, that Juliana of Cornillon was active in the church's adoption of the feast of Corpus Christi. Because of this the facts of her life have been preserved. One striking bit of information contained in her vita is that in 1197 she was placed in an Augustinian double monastery dedicated solely to the care of the sick and the lepers. More general sources of the period do not imply that there were Augustinian women in double monasteries doing such crucial social work. The sources are filled with stories about Franciscans and Dominicans doing social work, and that is as it should be, given the number of people involved in the mendicant movement and the number of people serving in Augustinian leper hospitals. We would be remiss, however, if we did not once again note the presence and importance of smaller houses, even while admitting that this is not the time or the place to identify them all. The Hospitallers of St. Gervais in Paris (f. 1171), the Canonesses Hospitallers of St. Catherine in Paris (f. 1222), the Hospitallers of Pontoise (f. 1259), the Trinitarians or Redemptors of Captives, and the Third Orders of Our Lady and of Servites are but a few of the better known small orders that flourished in France during this period, and there were likewise many small orders in Italy and in parts of Germany. Some orders established houses throughout Europe while still remaining small, as the Order of Penitents of St. Mary Madeleine (f. 1197) for reformed prostitutes did. Third orders were particularly popular as we enter into the Late Middle Ages; they offered women a way to combine a secular with a religious life in an age that saw an increased separation between the two.

6

The Visionary Late
Medieval Period

At mid-twentieth century many modern historians argued that one reason for the lackluster state of the church during the later Middle Ages was the lackluster condition within religious life. Today the historical validity of both presuppositions in this interpretation is subject to question. More recent historiography has shown that while the institutional church certainly suffered severe trauma, the devotional life of laypeople—"the church"—was vibrant, not dulled, and that religious societies, particularly religious societies for women, was likewise resplendent. In fact, there was so much energy and innovation emanating from women's religious societies that we are tempted to turn the discredited interpretation on its head: One reason for the vibrant state of the church during the Late Middle Ages was the sound condition of women's religious societies.

Immediately evident to the historian of women's religious societies is the variety of forms that this period created and nurtured. The uninitiated might read Boniface VIII's bull *Periculoso* and assume that it did indeed eliminate all types of religious life for women except enclosed monasticism. Quite the contrary is true, for numerous reasons. First, papal decrees were rarely if ever universally observed or even universally promulgated during this period. Second, there were no agreed-upon sanctions levied against anyone ignoring papal decrees, nor was it universally acknowledged that papal decrees were binding. While theologians readily admitted they owed obedience to papal decrees, there was a wide gap between what was expected of them and what was demanded of nontheologians — the people. Third, papal decrees often contradicted, overlapped, ignored, or altered previous papal decrees (for example, Innocent III's bull, *Privilege of Poverty* and Gregory IX's reissue), thus creating a "to-be-continued" mentality among the faithful, rather than an attitude that viewed papal bulls as the final word on a subject. Even when a bull was promulgated and understood, it was viewed as a general rule that most often was followed by bulls applying the general rule to individual cases. Numerous papal exemptions frequently followed each bull.

All this is not to say that the movement promoting enclosure of monastic women failed; to the contrary, it was overall a success. By the turn of the fourteenth century most already existing religious orders had embraced enclosure. However, many new orders, and even a few established before *Periculoso*, intentionally tried to bypass its strictures in order to engage in an active apostolate. In this sense *Periculoso* serves as a signpost for the study of women's religious life. After 1298, forms of religious life available to women develop more deliberately in two different directions: contemplative monastic communities lived in accordance with *Periculoso* and active service-oriented religious institutions structured to avoid enclosure. The former communities were always more officially recognized and respected, and hence they provided women with a socially sanctioned platform for leadership. The latter, however, were more dynamic and innovative, often helped determine the shape of the future, and rarely received official encouragement. Together these two types of religious life provided an atmosphere within which women flourished.

NEW FORMS OF RELIGIOUS LIFE

Tertiaries

The history of third orders is quite interesting. Tertiaries have been ignored as a general movement, although historians of individual religious orders have provided adequate surveys of the third order attached to those particular orders. Third orders became a canonically recognized branch of an approved religious order only after a long period of development and mutation. Some historians place the origins of third orders back with Benedictine oblates and with the informal associations many Benedictine monasteries formed with the laity in their vicinity. Other historians argue that the *vita apostolica* groups of the High Middle Ages were the first tertiaries. Still other historians claim that the vowed virgins of the fourth and fifth centuries in the East foreshadowed the tertiaries; the third orders also have been considered to be a type of pious lay fraternity like those fraternities that became so popular during the fourteenth and fifteenth centuries in Italian urban areas. The past is indeed replete with examples of individuals pledging themselves to a life similar in religious devotion and practice to monastic life, but lived outside a monastery.

By the thirteenth century the idea of a third order as a fraternity for people desirous of living an intense religious life while maintaining their secular status and role was an idea come of age. It was immensely popular and spread among the laity throughout the whole of Europe. The church never raised these third orders to a canonical status equivalent to religious orders, nor granted them the accompanying privileges, but in an age of increased laicization of society in general, such technicalities did little to dampen the people's desire to join. Often the clerical members of many religious groups tried to disassociate themselves with the third order, much as the new orders of the twelfth century tried to banish women from their religious families; Bonaventure (1221-1274), sometimes called the second founder of the Franciscans, believed that if "these Pentitents keep increasing they will hinder us and weaken our ability to help others; for they will think it is their right to have us always support them in every matter."[1] Such lack of welcome, however, did little to lessen the popularity of the life, which continued to grow throughout the rest of the medieval period.

The first of these groups to use the term *third order* was the *Humiliati,* and here is where we will start our discussion. The *Humiliati,* as mentioned earlier, were a *vita apostolica* group that was formally recognized by Innocent III in 1201 as orthodox. In 1200 they had organized themselves into what soon became the traditional three orders. The third order was often mentioned in the chronicles, indicating that contemporaries found this innovative *societas* (or *fraternitas,* or *universitas,* as various chroniclers called it) worthy of note. The laymen and laywomen members practiced the monastic virtues while living outside the monastery in their family homes. They dressed modestly, fasted, prayed, and served the poor. Innocent III granted them the unique privilege of preaching on non-theological matters among themselves at their Sunday meetings and the right to live under a rule separate from the first and second order.[2]

The *Humiliati* continued to exist as an organization throughout the century, but within a decade after papal approval attention and recruitment was focused elsewhere, as the Franciscans appeared on the scene.

When Francis of Assisi began his preaching mission, many people were not in a position to follow him as friars or nuns but still desired to live the life he prescribed. Historians are divided as to what happened next. Either Francis consciously established a third order and set down regulations for these laymen and laywomen, or the Franciscan name simply was attached to an already existing lay fraternity living the *vita apostolica*. Regardless, the first Franciscan lay group was called the Order of Pentitents, and it was very similar to the *Humiliati* third order. By 1221 it observed a rule that contained the usual norms of the *vita apostolica*—poverty, fasting, prayer, service to the poor—and had organized itself efficiently. Women had to obtain permission from their husbands to join.

The Dominican third order developed out of an amalgamation of groups belonging to the Order of Penitents that used Dominicans as their spiritual directors and members of a military order, Soldiers of Jesus Christ, founded to fight the Albigensians. In 1285 the tertiaries were given a formal rule by the master general of the Dominicans, Muñon de Zamora. The Carmelites, the third of the three great mendicant orders of the thirteenth century, had confraternities of tertiaries throughout Italy and France by the end of that century. But before the beginning of the fourteenth century an important development occurred within the third orders that altered their very nature: They began establishing traditional, enclosed communities.

Strange as this development may seem, it is understandable when events occurring in other forms of religious life, particularly in the life of beguines, are taken into consideration. During the course of the thirteenth century the beguines had endured much misunderstanding and frequently were accused of being heretical. They did not have an official rule and often were so informal that many groups bordered on disorganization. Adoption of the *Third Rule of St. Francis* addressed all the pressing issues, so many beguines did just that: They became tertiaries. This protected them from accusations of heresy, gave them a papally approved rule, and provided them with a scheme of organization. Communities of beguines in Strasbourg seem to be the first to become tertiaries, and the movement spread throughout Germany and the Low Countries by the turn of the century. Often the adoption signified little more than the beguinage's association with friars, but it did lead eventually to a distinction within third orders between third-order regulars (members who lived in a communal house and followed a *regula*, an approved rule) and third-order seculars (members who lived in the secular world).

The development of third orders was advantageous to women, for it gave them a type of protection by affiliation and a way of life that enabled them to make the most of their abilities. Some of the most powerful women of the era were members of a third order. Catherine of Siena (1347-1380) towers over all tertiaries in both power and importance. Drawn to an intense spiritual life, she fought her parents long and hard for permission to live out that religious life as a Dominican tertiary. She received the Dominican habit in 1365 and after three years of isolation and contemplation in her family home she embarked on a career of comprehensive reform with three goals: the first was to reform herself, "the second was for the reform of holy church, [and] the third was for the whole world in general."[3] Her reputation as a mystic and a social worker spread far and wide and eventually catapulted her into the center of international affairs as a mediator and arbitrator. While visiting Avignon in 1376 as Florence's peace negotiator with the papacy, Catherine became actively involved in efforts to get the papacy, which had moved to Avignon in 1305, to move back to Rome. She was successful in persuading Gregory XI to return, but her efforts to end the next scandal that plagued the institutional church, the Great Schism, were unsuccessful. When she died at age thirty-three the Dominican third order lost its greatest tertiary in an age of great women tertiaries.

Margaret of Cortona (1247-1297), sometimes called the third light of the Franciscan Order (Francis and Clare being the other two), repented of a life of sexual promiscuity, joined the third order, and enjoyed a rich mystical life. In 1286 she obtained a charter for a hospital, which she called Mary of Mercy. She then proceeded to found a congregation of tertiaries called Poverelle to staff the hospital as nurses and a confraternity to assist in all other hospital work. Emily of Vercelli's (1238-1314) family built and endowed what was probably the first Dominican third-order regular monastery; Emily was a renowned mystic and miracle worker. Angelina of Marsciano (1377-1435) established the first Franciscan third-order regular monastery. Angelina's group took vows and were enclosed; the popularity of the life led Angelina to found a total of sixteen such monasteries during her lifetime. One of the greatest mystical works of the Middle Ages was *The Book* by tertiary Angela of Foligno (1248-1309), often called *The Book of the Experience of True Faith*. Angela's spirituality was rooted in poverty and penance. "As it did not seem to me that there was any penance harsh enough to meet my need to break away from the world, I resolved then and there to give up absolutely everything and really do the kind of penance I felt called to do,"[4] Angela tells us. She further concluded that, as a married woman, she could best do this penance by following the dictates of the Franciscan third order. "And among other things she had asked Blessed Francis to ask God on her behalf to let her experience God's presence and likewise to obtain from him the grace of observing well the rule of Blessed Francis which she had recently promised; and above all she asked for this: that he would make her become, and remain to the end, truly poor."[5] Juliana Falconieri (1270-1341) became a tertiary in the newly founded Servite Order. She lived at home until her mother died in 1304, and then she moved into a communal home for religious women engaged in social work. (Because of their strenuous work they wore short sleeves; the nickname given to them because of this, "mantellate," became a term synonymous with all women tertiaries.) Shortly after joining Juliana composed a rule for women Servite tertiaries, and thus posterity has called her the founder of the female branch of the Servite Order. Joan Soderini (1301-1367), who succeeded Juliana as head of the order, was one of the most beloved and respected Servites of her day.

Clare of Montefalvo (d. 1308), famed mystic, lived as a Franciscan secular tertiary for fifteen years in a community led by her sister Joan. In 1290 the group decided they wanted to become third-order regulars, so they built the Monastery of the Holy Cross, adopted the *Rule of St. Augustine,* and made Clare their abbess. Mary of Cerevello (d.1290), called Mary of Help, was the first nun and prioress of the third-order regulars of the Order of Our Lady of Ransom (called Mercedarians), an order dedicated to ransoming Christian slaves from the Moors. Clare of Rimini (d.1346) joined the Franciscan third order at the beginning of her mystical life. When her husband died, her mystical life deepened and her active apostolate increased. Numerous women turned to her for spiritual direction, and she built them a monastery. She herself did not enter the monastery but remained a secular tertiary so she could continue her apostolic work. Clare was one of the most controversial mystics of her day; her public demonstrations (she had herself tied up and dragged through the streets during Holy Week) led many contemporaries to consider her mentally ill.

Tertiaries also included many famed members of royalty. Isabel of Portugal (1271-1336), daughter of Peter III, king of Aragon, and wife of Denis, king of Portugal, was a model for apostolic workers. She used her position to found charitable institutions, including an orphanage, a hospital at Coimbra, and a house for reformed prostitutes. Toward the end of her life she became a Franciscan tertiary. Elizabeth of Hungary (1207-1231), daughter of the King of Hungary, great-aunt of Isabel of Portugal, and often called the patron of the Franciscan third order, may not have actually ever joined the third order, but her actions, associations, and practiced virtues were all steeped in Franciscan ideals. By the time she died at age twenty-four she was esteemed throughout northern Europe for her charity. But perhaps the most beloved tertiary was the deformed, blind Margaret of Citta-di-Castello (1287?-1320) in Italy. Her parents were unable to accept their daughter's limitations and abandoned her in Citta-di-Castello, where the inhabitants soon adopted her after she won them over with her kindness and charity. Her cult was immensely popular during the Late Middle Ages.

Sisters of the Common Life

As the preceding discussions make clear, tertiaries and beguines had much in common. Both forms of life touched a cord to which women were highly responsive. Both forms accepted and appealed to all classes of people. Both types of religious life were quite compatible with the growing urban culture of the day, and both provided an approved form of religious life without enclosure. One more form of religious life created during this period shared all these characteristics: the Sisters of the Common Life.

Geert Groote (1340-1384) was a formidable man whose life reflected many of the prevailing movements of the day. He was highly educated, strongly influenced by mysticism, committed to charitable work, and actively engaged in church reform. His challenge was to create one single form of life that would allow and foster the types of behavior necessary to sustain education, mysticism, social work, and reform. In 1374 he gave his house in Deventer to a group of poor women. They gradually evolved from almshouse dwellers to a religious community that became the basis for the Sisters of the Common Life and eventually for the Brethren of the Common Life, established after Groote's death by a disciple, Florens Radewijns (1350-1400).

Like the beguines and the tertiaries, the Sisters of the Common Life imitated much in monastic life and eliminated much. They took no monastic vows but adhered to the spirit of those vows while they resided in the communal house. They could leave the community at will but could not return thereafter. They were members of the parish wherein their house lay, and they "dressed so poorly and commonly that when seen by some person of the world with little understanding of the things of God he usually mocks rather than honors them."[6] Great emphasis was placed on manual labor. "If you wish to achieve a truly spiritual life, you must refrain from too much talking, especially during manual labor," wrote Mother Salome Sticken (1369-1449), "because work is a kind of medicinal plaster for the wound of our sins. . . . [L]et me tell you that in all my life I never felt so affected toward the Lord as what I sensed when, still strong in body, I went out to the common labor."[7] They were self-supporting, with most members of the community working in the dairy and cloth industries. Their spiritual life was bolstered by charitable works, reading, and prayer, and marked by a practical mysticism.

In 1400 a foundation was made in Diepenveen for aspiring members (including this time wealthy women), and by the first years of the fifteenth century there were four more houses in Deventer, some in Utrecht, Delft, and Leiden, and others in most urban centers in the Low Countries. Documentation is scarce, but for the next half century houses for the Sisters of the Common Life showed up everywhere, almost overnight. No exact numbers for membership in all the sister houses is known, but we know that the sister house in 's-Hertogenbosch had five hundred sisters, built an annex to hold another two hundred, and at the same time founded other sister houses in Bommel, Rossum, Wamel and Birskt.

The Sisters were not always welcomed with open arms because their presence posed a labor problem. They worked hard and long and for low wages, which made them popular among employers but not among the employees, and they sold cloth goods for less than many conventional manufacturers. Complaints soon led to discussion within the sister houses and among the hierarchy about the wisdom of remaining outside the protection of canon law—of not living by an approved religious rule. One by one the sister houses adopted first the Franciscan and then the Augustinian rule. Thus we find a paradoxical situation at the turn of the century of a lay sisterhood attracting droves of women even while they were turning themselves into monastics. This changed their status drastically in the eyes of the world and may be partially responsible for the demise of the Sisters of the Common Life, which was as quick and complete as was their rise. The last known foundation was 1466, and before long they disappeared from sources and their historical significance diminished.

OLD FORMS OF RELIGIOUS LIFE

By the fourteenth century a traditional monastic order meant an enclosed order, but "enclosed" did not mean "sterile." Traditional monasticism was alive and well. Although we do not have accurate numbers of members for the period, we can safely surmise that they were very small. Only in England do reliable records enable estimates for membership, and here we know that ca. 1320 there were only two thousand women religious in monasteries. But conditions in England were unusual, for, as monastic scholar David Knowles has observed, "from the mid-thirteenth century onwards there was a dearth of founders and saints in England." No new orders, no new branches of orders, no monastic reform, no inspired preacher or saint or mystic "penetrate[d] to this country," as they did in all other countries.[8] Numbers elsewhere may have been significantly higher; records indicate but do not definitely prove that Germany had a much larger percentage of their women in traditional monasteries. We know that Strasbourg in 1257 had twelve enclosed monasteries with almost three hundred women and that there were thirty-two new Dominican monasteries founded in Germany between 1245 and 1251.[9] Whatever the actual total number, these women did have an impact on their society. Many reform movements initiated by women on the continent during the period had a great impact. Clara Gamacorta of Pisa (1362-1419) and Mary Mancini of Pisa (d. 1431) were two such reformers. They were acquaintances and correspondents of Catherine of Siena. Mary joined the Dominican third order after the death of her second husband. She later entered and then reformed a Dominican monastery but was still dissatisfied until she decided to join a new austere monastery built for Clara Gambacorta by her father. Following Catherine of Siena's advice to "use your time either by prayer, or reading, or by manual labor,"[10] the two founded a model community in 1382, from which a reform movement was born.

The Colettines: The Reform of the Poor Clares

The most successful reform movement occurred within the Poor Clares, under the leadership of Colette of Corbie (1381-1447). Its uniqueness lies in its being a reform movement initiated within the female branch of an order that spread into the male branch. When we look at Colette's life we can appreciate both the alternatives that women desirous of religious life had and the experimental temperament of the age as all searched for new forms of religious life to fit the new culture. Colette began as a beguine or tertiary in Picardy, but transferred to the enclosed monastery of the Poor Clares at Moncel when she realized she wanted to live a more austere life. This too was not enough for her, so next she tried the life of an anchorite. She was content living thus for about four years, but in 1406 Colette received visions that instructed her to reform the three orders of St. Francis. She determined she must found a new monastery of Poor Clares but also knew she needed hierarchical approval if she was to accomplish her goal of reform. She enlisted the aid of Henri de Baume, her new confessor and spiritual director, and set off to obtain papal permission for the experiment, depending on the authority of her visions and her spiritual director to help persuade the Pope. In 1406 Benedict XIII replied thus:

> The sincerity of your devotion towards us and the Roman church merits that we receive your demands favorably. Inflamed with zeal for religion and a fervor for devotion, you propose to found and to build someplace in the dioceses of Amiens, Paris or Noyons a monastery of enclosed nuns of the Order of St. Clare approved by our blessed predecessor Pope Innocent IV for you and certain virgins desiring to serve the Lord. . . . Furthermore, by virtue of the apostolic authority we presently hold, we give to this same monastery, after it has been built, and to all people living there now and in the future all the privileges, general and particular, all the indulgences and all the graces that can be granted by this authority.[11]

The actual foundation proved more difficult than Colette envisioned, but by 1408 her reformed monastery was a reality. In 1412 the new monastery received land in Auxonne to build a second one. Colette turned to the nearby friars' house at Dole for help, and in the process persuaded them to become part of her Franciscan reform movement; the First Order of St. Francis was now involved. During the course of the next two decades Colettine (Second Order) and Colettan (First Order) reform houses were established throughout France. By 1434 Colette believed the monasteries needed a set rule to abide by and so submitted a rule to the Franciscan minister general, William of Casal, for approval, which he gave: "I have received your letters, and spoken to your confessor concerning the approbation of the statutes you have sent and caused to be presented to me, which . . . at first appeared to me somewhat difficult. . . . At length I was persuaded . . . that the above named statutes were the particular work of God. Wherefore we resolve not only to confirm them but, moreover, to approve and promulgate them. . . ."[12] William had given the rule to "the Lord Cardinals of the Holy Cross and of Saint Angelo, Apostolic legates and at this time actually Presidents at the Council of Basel, and many doctors of Sacred theology and venerable Fathers very famous of life and learning."[13] Still, the women wanted more; they wanted their constitutions to "be supported by the Apostolic authority for their greater stability."[14] Pius II responded not only with confirmation but "at the same time withdrawing, recalling and annulling every and singular" document from the hierarchy "by which any derogation should seem to be made."[15]

All this dotting of the i's and crossing of the t's may account for the success and speed of the reform. Colette had removed any possible objection local clergy might have to the presence of her monasteries. The movement spread to the Low Countries, Italy, and Germany. The Franciscans were never known as a peaceful family, however, and fights and jealousies soon erupted between the Observant friars and the Colettan friars. The Colettines, however, were not so disrupted, and they continued to flourish. The order nurtured many women of note during the fifteenth century. Felicia Meda (1378-1444) of Milan founded a famous monastery in Pesaro. Camilla Varani (b. 1449) was a noted mystic and author. Antonia of Florence (d. 1476?) was at first a member of one of sixteen Franciscan third-order monasteries founded by the famed Angelina of Marsciano (1377-1435), but in 1447 she founded a new monastery under the stricter Colettine constitution. Her Corpus Christi Monastery was one of the more cultured and popular monasteries of the day. Catherine of Bologna (1413-1463), close companion of Margaret d'Este, daughter of the ruling family of Ferrara, was a third-order regular who had her house adopt the Colettine reform. She is best remembered for her many spiritual writings, hymns, paintings, and especially for her illuminated breviary.

The Bridgettines: Order of the Holy Savior

Reformation of existing orders was not the only activity going on within traditional monasticism during the Late Middle Ages; some new orders were being formed. For the most part they stayed within the staid boundaries that defined monasticism since the days of Benedict, with perhaps a twist here and there. Santuccia Terrebotti (1258-1305) was abbess of a Benedictine monastery in Gubbio until she was offered an opportunity to relocate in Rome in an abandoned Templars' building. There she altered their way of life just enough to warrant their being called the Order of the Servants of Mary.

The most successful new traditional order of the period likewise offered little innovation. What it did offer was the resurrection of an older form of monasticism that had been forgotten of late, the double monastery. Bridget (Birgitta) of Sweden (1303?-1373), mystic, author, prophet, politician, wife, mother, social worker, and theologian, was the founder of the Order of the Holy Savior, commonly known as the Bridgettines. A contemporary of Catherine of Siena, Bridget was as fascinating and multifaceted a figure as her fellow mystic, and together they shared a unique degree of fame, influence, and power. In an age of institutional ecclesiastical chaos the mystical message and spiritual presence of both Catherine of Siena and Bridget of Sweden dominated.

Bridget was born of wealthy, powerful parents in Finsta Gaard and was summarily educated and married by age thirteen. After twenty years of a happy marriage and eight children, she was summoned to court to head the king's household. When her husband died in 1344, Bridget immediately "distributed all her goods among her children and the poor. She changed her way of living and dressing."[16] Bridget had long desired these changes in behavior, which were rooted in visions she had received a few years prior to her husband's death. One of the first ones, probably received while on pilgrimage with her husband to Santiago de Compostella around 1339-1340, concerned the foundation of a new monastery for women in atonement for the sins of the Swedes, and built on the king's land.

> When Jesus Christ appeared to me and began to speak, I confess that in a very brief time all the articles of this rule with all the words which it contained were dictated to me. It was not as if the words were written down on paper, but as if I miraculously heard them and was able to comprehend them. I hid them somewhere in my subconscious. . . . After a few days with them in my heart I told them to a religious man, a friend of God, who quickly wrote them all down.[17]

She was then "instructed in spirit to go to the king of Sweden" for his permission to found this monastery, "and when she pleaded the excuse that she did not know what to say to him, this answer was made to her by God: 'When you arrive,' he said, 'open your mouth and I will fill it.'"[18]

Her words were persuasive and King Magnus agreed to seek ecclesiastical approval for the project. He allowed his castle of Vadstena to become the site for her monastery in 1346, but construction was halted in 1348 because papal confirmation of her rule had just been refused on the grounds that the Fourth Lateran Council of 1215 had forbidden the foundation of any more new religious orders that did not adopt an already existing monastic rule. When Bridget fell out of favor at court in 1349 due to internal politics, her visions told her that now was the time to go to Rome to seek approval of her order in person. To make sure she could plead her case eloquently, she learned Latin, and then departed for Rome sometime in 1350. She remained there until her death in 1373.

Once in Rome Bridget became involved in much more than simply getting her new rule accepted. She immediately became engaged in the politics of the day and tried to facilitate the return of the Avignon papacy to Rome, to reform monasteries in Farfa and Bologna, and to influence policy back in Sweden. She traveled, made pilgrimages, performed charitable works, and recorded the readings for her order's daily office (these being revealed to her in visions). Her fame spread far and wide. Years passed as she waited for the papacy's return to Rome from its Babylonian Captivity in Avignon. In vain the reigns of Clement VI (1342-1352) and Innocent VI (1352-1362) passed. Finally Urban V (1362-1370) returned briefly and was given the rule, but he left the city once again without passing judgment on it. Bridget was not at all satisfied with this situation, as the following visionary message reveals:

> The Son of God said to his bride: "He who has a ball of thread which has the best gold inside does not abandon the ball until he finds the gold. The owner of the gold uses it to his honor and advantage. Pope Urban is gold that can be led to good, but he is hemmed in by worldly preoccupations. Therefore go and tell him on My behalf: your time is short. Rise and look at how the souls that have been entrusted to you can be saved. I have brought you the rules of the order that has to be founded and begun in Sweden, at Vanstena. It has come forth from My mouth. Now I want you not only to confirm it through a mandate, but also to strengthen it through your blessing, you who are My vicar on earth. I have dictated it and endowed it with spiritual endowment. . . . You must approve publicly, in front of men, that which has been sanctified in the presence of My heavenly assembly. . . ." But you, My bride, to whom I have conceded the aforesaid privilege, if you cannot get the pope's letter, favor and seal for the concession of the indulgences, except by buying it beforehand, My blessing is more than enough for you.[19]

In other words, by 1370 her patience was wearing thin, and Bridget wanted an answer. She did get one, but it was not exactly the one she wanted. Claiming that the dictates set by the Fourth Lateran Council forbidding the approval of new rules must be observed, Urban agreed that Bridget could found her Order of the Holy Saviour, but that the order must adopt the *Rule of St. Augustine* (a rule approved before the Fourth Lateran Council) and use Bridget's own rule only as a supplement. To say that Bridget was not happy with Urban's answer is an understatement: "If he should succeed in getting back to his own country [France] he will be struck such a blow that his teeth will shake in his mouth. . . . The friends of God will no longer include him in their prayers, and he will be called to account to God for what he did and what he did not do."[20]

In the remaining three years of her life Bridget seems to have given up her dream for the order as she originally envisioned it. It is mentioned only one more time, in the last chapter of her last *Book of Revelation,* just before her death: "'Thus I have not visited you with consolations during this time, for it was the time of your testing. Therefore, now that you have already tested, go forward and prepare yourself; for now is the time for the fulfillment of that which I promised you: namely, that before my altar you shall be clothed and consecrated as a nun. And henceforth you shall be counted not only as My bride, but also as a nun and a mother in Vadstena.'"[21]

Upon Bridget's death, her daughter Catherine and Peter of Alvastra accompanied her body home to Vadstena where the monastery and the church were built according to Bridget in her *Revelations.* In 1378, thanks to her daughter, Urban VI issued final approval of the Order of the Holy Saviour and gave Bridget's rule equal weight alongside that of Augustine's. Vadstena quickly became both the spiritual and cultural center of northern Europe. The order spread slowly, but by the beginning of the fifteenth century Bridgettine monasteries were found in Italy, Denmark, Norway, Germany, and Poland. In England the brightest star of the Bridgettine Order, the Monastery of Syon, was founded in 1415. Syon played a major role in the religious history of England right up to the Dissolution of the Monasteries during the Reformation, the act of Henry VII that closed all English monasteries.

The story of Bridget's life and of her conception of a women's religious order contains some of the boldest challenges to the male ecclesiastical authority to date. First, she claimed her rule was a revealed rule. Contemporaries chafed at the premise behind such a belief. As an adversary during Bridget's canonization process wrote ca. 1382: "There are many saints of great devotion and authority in the church, such as Benedict, Basil, Francis and many others, who composed rules . . . yet Christ by his own mouth dictated to none of these. Why did he dictate to [Bridget] rather than the others?"[22] The answer given by Adam Easton, the defender of Bridget during the canonization process, reveals that all were aware of what was really being argued: Why dictate a rule to a woman? God did this "so that to both sexes of mankind he would give the privileges of his grace."[23] Bridget's rule, after all, was "general and rude in style and so defective," but that was necessary because "nuns or women are weak in intellect and . . . more unlearned in the capacity for doctrine and more simple than men."[24]

Second, the structure of Bridget's order was bold in its assertion of female dominance. Each monastery was to contain "the sixty sisters, the thirteen priests, the four deacons and eight of their servants so that the total number of persons is equal to the thirteen apostles and seventy-two disciples."[25] It was the abbess, however, who is "the head and the mistress" of all eighty-five religious and "she shall be consulted in all that pertains to the business and to the monastery." It is also the abbess who must "elect one of the thirteen priests as a confessor to all," whom they "must obey in everything," but the confessor himself is still under the authority of the abbess and cannot do anything without first consulting with her.[26] The basis for this claim of authority was Bridget's understanding of the relationship between Mary and her Son, as dictated by Christ. "The abbess is elected by the convent, with the bishop's counsel. Out of reverence to the Most Blessed Virgin, my mother, to whom this order is dedicated, the abbess is head and ruler, just as the Virgin herself, like the abbess on earth, became head and queen of my apostles and disciples after ascending with me into heaven."[27] In other words, the salvation of Swedish men and women is to be accomplished by the foundation of a female-ruled religious order that would eliminate the need for any other order: Women are critical in the redemption of Sweden. "But Christ appeared to woman first for this reason, that as a woman was first to bring the source of death to man, so she might be the first to announce the dawn of Christ's glorious resurrection."[28] As Adam Easton writes, "And the same causes can be given, that, just as the evil teaching came by a woman [Eve], so the rule for good living would come to others by a woman."[29]

Because the ecclesiastical world was obviously not composed entirely of Adam Eastons, Bridget's vision was never fully realized. Certain gains were made, but certain rights also were held back. "Considering the frailty of their sex, it is fitting," wrote Pius II in his bull confirming Colette of Corbie's reformed constitutions for the Poor Ladies, "that we shelter them in the embrace of our paternal arms, accounting this to be most expedient for them."[30] Bridget would have disagreed; considering the frailty of both sexes, all should be sheltered in the embrace of her order's maternal arms.

7

The Reformation Era

The Late Middle Ages is one of the more complex periods in Western culture. It is filled with so many ups and downs, so many contradictory and so many paradoxical situations, that the historian can write a negative or a positive assessment of the era and be able to support either thesis with pages of documentation. It was an age of Renaissance as well as plague, discovery as well as decay. Recent work in women's history has served only to further complicate any attempt at a simple interpretation of the period. Joan Kelly Gadol's provocative and influential article, "Did Women Have a Renaissance?"[1] examined property relations, literature, and political and social institutions to document her thesis that Italy from 1350 to 1530 was a regressive period for women. Carolyn Walker Bynum's equally provocative work, *Holy Feast and Holy Fast*,[2] studies religious symbolism, pietistic writings, and material culture to support her thesis that the period provided a significant number of opportunities for women. The history of women religious likewise indicates that this was a positive period for women.

Besides the fact that institutionalized religious life was available to women in more forms, it was also available to more women. The third orders were open to the poor and the rich alike, and they attracted vast numbers from both classes. The beguines were so popular among the lower class that they attracted the attention of the upper class. The Sisters of the Common Life originally required that members be poor, but their success and popularity made the upper class clamor for admission. With the expansion of kinds of, and membership in, institutionalized religious life, more women of diverse backgrounds had access to positions of authority within the religious groups. When the records of the women's monasteries in the diocese of Norwich, England, from this period are examined, they reveal that merit and ability, not social status, were the key to positions of authority.[3] This is in marked contrast with the Anglo-Saxon monasteries of old where the aristocracy held a near monopoly on monastic offices. More and more the leadership of women's communities reflected the social composition of the communities, and the social composition was increasingly middle class, particularly in newer communities.

There were, of course, negative aspects present in women's religious communities in the pre-Reformation period. Many older monastic communities were in sore need of revival. Membership in the Sisters of the Common Life, the beguines, and the tertiaries was declining by the mid-fifteenth century, and the decreased presence of these women created a gap. During the course of the sixteenth century women labored with dogged determination to fill that gap with permanent institutions that embodied the spirit and goals of the disappearing forms of religious life created earlier.

THE ACTIVE WOMEN RELIGIOUS

One of the developments occurring in secular society, however, played a role in women's creation of the new orders. During the Late Middle Ages the whole legal system entered into a phase of tremendous growth and sophistication. The birth of representative institutions, the creation of new courts, the genesis of new state bureaucracy, and the extension of law into previously unregulated areas of behavior combined to produce a somewhat legalistic age, or at least a society conscious of legal ramifications. In the world of religious communities this had great impact, and only after the dilemmas caused by the canonical status of women's religious communities were solved were women free to create the type of religious communities they truly desired.

Specifically, what was at issue was the classification of woman religious in canon law and, consequently, in secular law. Women who publicly took the vows prescribed by a papally approved religious rule were recognized in canon law as separate from the laity. This meant that they had privileges and obligations above and beyond what laywomen had, that they had a distinct relationship with the hierarchy, and that this unique relationship was acknowledged by the secular courts. After 1298 and the bull *Periculoso* it meant that they were supposed to be enclosed. But it also meant that society, both secular and ecclesiastical, afforded them special consideration and respect. The importance of the respect in particular is hard to overestimate. Herein lies the dilemma: If women wanted to live in nonenclosed communities, then they could not take solemn vows (these publicly taken vows, from which dispensations were rarely granted, annulled all rights to ownership of money and property and were recognized in civil as well as in canon law) and live under an approved rule. If they did not take solemn vows, then they were still legally members of the laity and therefore not entitled to society's special consideration or respect. Canon law could not offer them protection or immunity from secular law or exemption from taxes and dues.

The question of canonical status was of particular concern in matters that feudal law also dealt with. Feudal law determined the inheritance laws, which in turn determined the economic position of each woman and ultimately, via the dowry, the economic health of each religious community. In canon and feudal law, a woman entering a religious community had the right to bring her inheritance with her for the community's use. A woman entering a lay community did not. Much of the indecision and the ambivalence that the hierarchy and society in general displayed toward new communities of women dedicated to apostolic work was due to the complications brought about by these facts. A woman who joined an active community could take only simple vows (privately taken vows that possibly could be dispensed with and that left ownership rights intact) if she wished to avoid enclosure. At first both the women and the hierarchy thought simple vows the perfect compromise, and so during the fifteenth and early sixteenth century active communities with simple vows were founded and approved. Once the ramifications of skirting feudal inheritance laws were realized, however, there was a strong reaction against such communities, and pressure was put on their members to take solemn vows and become enclosed.

It was too late, however, for a return to an age gone by. Society found that it now had too great a need for dedicated social workers, and, more to the point, feudal inheritance laws themselves were being abandoned and replaced. Within a few generations of the church's rejection of the active orders, the hierarchy once more reversed itself, this time permanently, and permitted the existence of nonenclosed women religious. The church at first avoided the issue by using new terms such as congregation and institute to replace the traditional term religious order, but by the time it did, people no longer cared. Seventeenth-century society did not embrace the legalistic mentality or the feudal law of the fifteenth and sixteenth centuries. By the end of seventeenth century the whole of society implicitly acknowledged that there were two distinct types of women's religious communities: active and contemplative. Both types were equally deserving of society's special consideration and respect.

The journey to full acceptance of women's active orders was long, tedious, and anything but direct. It began in the thirteenth century and ended in the seventeenth century, but the most intense period of activity was from the early fifteenth century to the early seventeenth century.

The Oblates of Tor de' Specchi

That more and more women drawn to religious life during the course of the Late Middle Ages also were attracted to a life of service was documented in Chapter 6. Given the developments in Western society, such vocations are understandable. As cities grew and division of labor increased, a void arose in society that needed to be filled: an institution responsible for the sick and the needy. The women who founded the new religious communities of the era were women who correctly perceived the situation and offered a solution.

One of the earliest and more successful individual responses to the call for service and religious life was articulated by Frances of Rome (1384-1440). Frances was a very admirable figure of Roman nobility, and even as a young bride of thirteen she was held in high regard. Her marriage was a happy one. Her husband Lorenzo, when not wounded, or a prisoner, or in exile due to civil conflicts in Rome, was her dearest companion and true soulmate. She likewise shared similar social and spiritual desires with her sister-in-law Vannozza, who, together with Frances and Lorenzo lived with Lorenzo's permissive parents. They allowed the two women to engage in social work outside the house, an uncommon activity for women of their social standing. Soon Frances and Vannozza agreed to live a strict regulated life. They built two small oratories in the garden and in the house, adhered to a schedule of prayer, and spent all their spare time in charitable work, especially in nursing at the Hospital of San Spirito.

For the next few decades Frances mothered three children, ran the family estate, lived through wars, and continued her active apostolate. Her husband ceded her complete control over her own actions and person in exchange for a promise that she would live with him until his death. After her husband's liberating gesture Frances began making plans with a small group of women whose model and guide she was, to form a kind of third order attached to a neighborhood Benedictine monastery. In 1425 the plans became reality when Frances and nine companions were received officially in the Benedictine Order of Mt. Olivet as Oblates of Mary. For seven years they were bound together as oblates living at home, until Frances decided that "as we have been united in spirit and in intention, so ought we to be in our outward mode of life."[4] She declared that it was the Lord's will "that I should found a new spiritual edifice in this city, the ancient stronghold of religion and faith. It will form an asylum for those persons of your sex and of your rank who have conceived the generous resolution of forsaking the world and its allurements."[5] In 1432 they were able to buy a house for the new order in a section of town called Tor de' Specchi, and when they took possession in March 1432, they became known as the Oblates of Tor de' Specchi.

Faithful to her promise to Lorenzo, she did not reside in the new community house, but she did occupy herself with writing a constitution and rule for the group. Finally, after forty years of marriage, Lorenzo's death freed Frances to join the community she had founded, and four days after entering she was made superior of the community by order of her confessor-spiritual director and the community's protector, Giovanni Mattiotti. The Oblates' life was divided among community prayer, mediation, reading, and social work. They did not take vows, wore the dress of the day, and were not enclosed. They applied to the papacy for the right to live as a community, to elect their own superior, to have that superior choose the community's confessor, and to conduct liturgy in their own chapel. The hierarchy's response was mixed. They did not allow the women to choose their own superior, but instead placed them under the jurisdiction of the monks at San Maria Nuova. In 1444 the papacy extended to their group other privileges and made it plain that the monks were not to control the women. During the following years both Oblates and monks jockeyed for position, and it was quite a few decades before the women's struggle for independence was completely victorious. Their immense popularity among the people of the city, the poor and the powerful alike, did much to assure the Oblates' victory. Many other groups of women religious were formed in the city at this time, groups such as the Mantellate of St. Monica, founded by the rich noblewomen Margarita Bartelluti. These groups were established about the same time as Frances was forming her group, but the Oblates of Tor de' Specchi were the most successful of all the experiments in noncloistered religious life for Italian women.

The story of Frances would be incomplete if mention were not made of the role her confessor-spiritual director played in the acceptance of the Oblates within the ecclesiastical world. At each stage of Frances' journey toward the foundation of the Oblates, permission was granted by those in control for her to proceed further in part because she had the backing of Giovanni Mattiotti. Here we see the beginning of a trend that would culminate in the post-Reformation era. As women tried to remove the barriers within which their activities were confined, they needed allies. During the thirteenth and fourteenth centuries visions were used to accomplish this; the mystic who could persuade the hierarchy that the authority of God was directly behind her demands met little resistance — consider Catherine of Siena and most Italian tertiary saints. In the latter part of the fourteenth century, as the mystical movement became so widespread that it perhaps also became diluted, women turned elsewhere for help. The figure of the confessor-spiritual director was just evolving in the West at this time, and he proved to be a most helpful advocate for women desirous of noncloistered religious life.

The Grey Sisters

Perhaps because the Oblates of Tor de' Specchi were ahead of their time, or perhaps because only urban areas had a great need for them, Frances' community did not blossom into an international order. It remained a brilliant but solitary light in Rome for generations and eventually a source of inspiration for women of later generations interested in apostolic work. Another group of women whose community prospered and grew in the direction of a fully international active order was that of the Third Order Franciscan Hospitallers, known under numerous names but chiefly as the Grey Sisters. Their origins have much in common with other third-order groups already discussed, but those aspects distinguishing them from other third orders are significant enough historically to warrant individual attention here.

A group of women who had earlier formed an association dedicated to helping the poor and the sick found it advantageous in 1388 to become affiliated with the Franciscan third order. These women, best known for their nursing, were so appreciated that they were rarely in need of financial support or members. They spread throughout France and the Low Countries during the fifteenth century and had approximately one hundred houses by 1500. During most of the fifteenth century the houses founded were independent of each other, a situation that many Grey Sisters wanted to change. In 1483 the superiors of twenty-four houses met, along with John Crohin, the Franciscan Observant Provincial Vicar of France, and Jacques Stoetlin, designated visitor of the Hospitallers, to compose statutes for all Grey Sisters and thus mold them into a distinct religious order. Examination of the statutes reveals their historical significance: They are the oldest known rules for a women's active religious community.

The life the women led is easily gleaned from the statutes. Novices had to be between the ages of seventeen and thirty. They promised "to live in obedience, poverty and chastity, and to follow the Third Rule of St. Francis."[6] Members' prayer life revolved around the community mass and the recitation of the Little Office of the Holy Virgin (an abbreviated version of the monastic Divine Office), which was adjusted to the needs of the four seasons. They clearly thought their apostolic work was of equal spiritual value to their prayer life, for they were excused from the Office if their work demanded their presence elsewhere. Indeed, if a superior noticed that a woman preferred the contemplative life to the active life, the superior was to force the woman back to her nursing duties. The Grey Sisters maintained their own hospitals but did much of their nursing in the homes of the sick. To avoid possible scandal while performing what they acknowledged was groundbreaking activity for women, they traveled in pairs to the homes, rotated partners and jobs weekly, did not eat with their patients' families, and coordinated their work with the parish clergy.

Another order that had similar origins but a different ending was the Bernardine Sisters of the Franciscan third order. In 1457 a group of women tertiaries moved into St. Agnes' Monastery in Cracow and occupied themselves with much charitable work. They cared for the elderly and the sick and instructed the poor during the first decades of their existence, but eventually they abandoned the work to become a fully contemplative community. They continued to thrive into modern times, and after spreading to North America in 1894 they reverted to their original purpose of nursing and instructing.

The Ursulines

The Grey Sisters were successful in attaining a goal that had escaped many others: They were an approved religious order that was permitted to pursue a life of service outside the monastery. Like the Oblates of Tor de' Specchi, however, they did not capture the imagination of the day and enjoyed only modest popularity. Perhaps their identity as a third-order regular Franciscan community, a common enough association, blinded people to the uniqueness of their situation. That certainly was not the case for the next major active order to emerge in the West, the Ursulines. Everything about them caught their contemporaries' attention: the personality of their founder, the novelty of their activities, their way of life, and their success. And their history always has caught historians' attention, because they, perhaps more than any other order, embodied all the conflicts and complexities of the issues present in women's religious communities during the early modern period.

Their founder, Angela Merici (1470/74-1540), grew up in Desenzano, Lombardy, in a family of modest means. Orphaned at an early age, Angela lived with her uncle in Salo until age twenty-two, when she returned to Desenzano and began her career as a teacher. At some point she joined the Franciscan third order, and soon fellow tertiaries joined in her apostolate. She established a school that was a quiet success, and the Franciscans grew to recognize her potential. In 1516 they sent her to Brescia on a charitable errand, and she ended up staying there for the rest of her life.

Brescian society was very much involved in the reform movement that was only simmering in 1516 but within a decade would soon boil over into the Reformation. Prior to Luther's stance at Wittenberg and the ensuing Protestant Reformation, Spain and Italy had given rise to the Catholic Reformation. One of the achievements of this reform movement was the creation of lay charitable associations for men throughout Italy. In Brescia the members of one confraternity, the Company of Divine Love, made it their mission to minister to those who suffered from a disease newly arrived in the West, syphilis. Given the nature of the venereal disease, the men came in contact with many prostitutes. Quickly realizing that these sick women were best ministered to by other women, a women's auxiliary of sorts arose to complement the work of the men's Company. Wealthy Brescian women already were involved in rescuing poor women from destitute situations that encouraged prostitution, so this was considered to be merely an extension of their original apostolate. It served, however, as an impetus to form a more permanent and a more independently recognized women's lay group. Angela was at the center of the movement to establish these women in a formal, independent association. Her apostolate when she arrived in Brescia was a continuation of her apostolate in Desenzano, that of religious education, and so now she combined her original interest with the new need. She drew around her eight women interested in offering religious education to diseased and unschooled poor women. Together they formed an association to fulfill that apostolate.

The organization of the group was brilliant. Angela used her knowledge of the times to fashion a comprehensive rule that anticipated most possible criticisms. Members of her group, now called the Company of St. Ursula, came from humble origins, so she involved the upper class by asking the townswomen to serve as lady governors of the Company and the townsmen to assist in temporal affairs as protectors of the Company. She adopted the municipal plan of Brescia as the administrative model of the Company; Brescia's eight administrative sections became the Company's eight neighborhoods. As each of the town's administrative sections enjoyed some local autonomy, so too each of the Company's neighborhoods practiced a degree of self-government. Every neighborhood had one lady governor overseeing it. The lady governor was to have "particular information about the members" in their neighborhood. They were to "know the name of each, her home and her family: they should be acquainted with her state and condition in life, her habits, her ways and her social environment, at home and elsewhere."[7] Before a woman even got to be a member, though, she was screened carefully. She

> must be a virgin . . . must enter gladly and of her own free will. Third, she must not be bound by any monastic vow, nor by engagements to any man in the world. Fourth, if she have father, mother or other guardians she must first ask their permission; after which the Governors of the Company should talk to her in order to discover if there be any legitimate impediment to her entering this holy obedience. Fifthly, she must be at least twelve years old when she presents herself, fifteen when she is invested and taken into the Chapter, and eighteen or twenty when she is professed.[8]

The stringent requirements and supervision of members were necessary, for the Company lived at home, clothed "modest and simple as truly befits a virginal modesty,"[9] and took no vows. Neighborhood meetings were held frequently so members could talk over any problems they had in juggling home life and religious life, or in carrying out their apostolate. Three mature women officers (a lady governor, an older assistant, and a novice mistress) of the neighborhood met "at least once a fortnight . . . to provide for the needs of members under their charge" and "to hold the neighborhood assembly at the stated time, examining into and providing for the wants of the members."[10] They were to send a report to the mother general of the whole Company after every neighborhood meeting.

Angela's caution was well conceived, because the Company of St. Ursula was quite innovative and therefore viewed with doubt. It was not meant to be a variation of the Oblates of Tor de' Specchi or the Grey Sisters. In fact, it originally was not intended to be a religious order. Angela desired no formal or canonical commitment, only permission to live under the mandate of the Company's rule. The Company's main purpose was to "carry on some charitable work, especially the work of Christian instruction,"[11] which was, at the same time, a work much needed and much debated. To many, women teachers were the answer to the pressing question of who was going to save the next generation from heterodoxy. To others, women teachers came dangerously close to conflicting with the scriptural prohibition of women preachers (1 Cor. 11, 2-16; 14:34-35; and 1 Tim. 2:11-12). Angela's adroit handling of the townspeople, the members, and the hierarchy, and the success of the women in the field, however, did much to ward off any real opposition, and the Company was soon an accepted and indispensable part of Brescian life. Episcopal approval of the Company was given in 1536, and four years after Angela's death (1544), Paul III promulgated a bull of approbation. Not only did he approve of the Company as a women's confraternity, but he extended the women's property rights beyond what was usual for confraternity members. Their rights were on par with those granted to members of a religious order: Members of St. Ursula's Company were "as much entitled to their inheritance portion as if they had entered the marriage state or some canonically erected monastery."[12]

A year after this bull was issued, the Council of Trent convened, and so began yet another alteration and even reversal of official ecclesiastical attitudes toward women's religious communities. During the centuries preceding Trent, we have seen that the hierarchy did not press energetically for compliance with Boniface VIII's mandate for enclosure of all women religious; the charitable needs of society and the religious needs of women were being quietly accommodated. In 1563 the Council disowned this benign acceptance and stated that it, "renewing the constitution of Boniface VIII which begins *Periculoso*, commands all bishops ... [to] make it their special care that in all monasteries subject to them ... the enclosure of nuns be restored wherever it has been violated and that it be preserved where it has not been violated; restraining with ecclesiastical censures and other penalties, every appeal being set aside, the disobedient and gainsayers, even summoning for this purpose, if need be, the aid of the secular arm."[13] But since the question of whether tertiaries, beguines, oblates, or confraternity members were nuns in the eyes of canon law was never answered, it was still a matter of debate whether they were included in this mandate for enclosure.

This precipitated a further clarification, the bull *Circa pastoralis*, promulgated in 1566 by Pius V. Here he demanded that female tertiaries and women living in community without observing enclosure either accept enclosure or disband, that all professed nuns take solemn vows, that solemn vows implicitly contain enclosure, and that any community that took simple vows rather than solemn vows not be allowed to accept any more members.[14] This document was followed in 1570 by yet another bull, *Decori*, in which Pius V tightened the criteria for acceptable reasons to leave a monastery; by the 1572 bull *Deo sacris* of Gregory XIII, which nullified Pius V's one exception for leaving a monastery, begging; by the 1575 bull *Ubi gratiae*, in which Gregory XIII restricted those who were to be granted permission to visit inside a monastery; and, finally, by the bull *Dubiis*, which was issued a few years later by Gregory XIII to further clarify his earlier bulls.

The papacy, as a review of the extensive legislation makes quite clear, was more serious than ever about women religious being enclosed. Based only on these facts, one would be justified in concluding that the hierarchy had struck a death blow at the heart of the movement to create active religious orders for women. The ammunition aimed at the attempts was overwhelming, and even after careful study it is not always clear exactly why the directives failed, or how the movement remained alive and eventually triumphed.[15] But triumph it did, although not immediately and not until religious communities like the Company of St. Ursula were radically altered.

The second phase of the history of Angela Merici's organization is the story of how the Company of St. Ursula was transformed into a religious order called the Ursulines. After Angela's death in 1540 subtle changes in the Company began to mold it more into a formal religious order. In 1546 the bishop of Brescia insisted that the women wear a distinctive religious habit rather than obey the rule's call for simple and modest dress. As the first-generation members of the Company grew old and ill, two wealthy Brescian women donated property to the Company for a home for the aged. When they took up residence there, de facto community life was made available to them. And when members began instructing youth in school settings instead of in their homes, the women viewed community life as a natural, convenient way to better dedicate all their energies to educating youth.

Changes of a more radical nature occurred when the Company expanded beyond Brescia. The women's accomplishments, which by the end of the first generation included extensive hospital work as well as education, were attracting attention throughout Europe. Charles Borromeo (1538-1584), archbishop of Milan, nephew of Pius IV, and one of the guiding forces of the Counter Reformation, was most interested in their work, for the women were already doing what post-Tridentine bishops had just realized had to be done. When Borromeo turned his reforming eyes to his archdiocese, he knew that any solution to the church's problems had to include instruction of the laity, and he also saw that Angela Merici and the Company had already perfected the methods and approaches needed to achieve such a goal. He invited the Company to send twelve women to Milan to teach along with his male catechists in his famous Confraternity of Christian Doctrine. Since the invited women could obviously not live with their families, he also offered to give them a house to live in. Although new members coming from Milan could live at home, according to the Brescian model, they rarely chose to do so, and from the women's arrival in 1568 the Company of St. Ursula in Milan was quite similar to other religious orders living a traditional communal life. In 1572 a series of changes compiled by Charles Borromeo were approved by Gregory XIII; these included the right to live a communal life but without enclosure. Ten years later Borromeo again revised the rule of the Milan Company, which by now was under his jurisdiction. In effect he remolded Angela's original Company into a religious order called the Ursulines, an order quite distinct from the Brescian Company. This ended any hope the women had of remaining a single religious institutional entity as they spread from city to city; instead, they were similar but jurisdictionally independent communities. They remain a great and admirable order today, but not in the form that Angela de Merici originally envisioned.

CONTEMPLATIVE WOMEN RELIGIOUS

While successful, innovative, and avant-garde experiments of one age tend to get more attention from historians if they dominate the subsequent age, it should be remembered that often this leads to an exaggerated sense of new institutions' contemporary importance. The fifteenth- and sixteenth-century experiments in women's active religious communities often were overshadowed in their contemporary world by the more familiar forms of religious life, and not merely because the traditional forms were better known. It was because traditional monastic communities were also stirring with activity.

Some of the activity was restricted to the establishment of female branches of new male orders. Catherine Colombini (d. 1387) was a cousin of the founder of the Jesuati, John Colombini (1304-1367); Catherine founded the women's branch, the Poor Jesuatesses of the Visitation of the Blessed Virgin Mary, in 1367. Frances d'Amboise (1427-1485) usually is designated as the cofounder of the Carmelite nuns, along with John Soreth, because of the expansion of the group under her leadership. Unlike the Carmelite men who were mendicants, the women were strictly enclosed. In 1506 a rule for women Minims, or Hermits of St. Francis of Assisi, was confirmed by papal bull, although the first women already had been received in the order in 1495. The women's group originated in Spain and followed almost exactly the same strict rule as the men. The Sisters of St. Ambrose ad Nemus were founded by Catherine Morigia (1438-1478), who in her desire to live a most austere life used the monks of St. Ambrose ad Nemus as her inspiration. Maria Garcìas (d.1426) founded the women's branch of the Jeronymites, or Hermits of St. Jerome, in Toledo in the early fifteenth century, although they were not formally incorporated into the order until 1510. The Spanish widow Maria Laurentia Longo founded the Capuchin Sisters of the Order of St. Clare in Naples. Sometimes called the Daughters of the Passion, they were officially approved and placed under the direction of the Capuchin Fathers, a reform Franciscan order, in 1538. Two orders of Theatine nuns were founded by Ursula Bennincasa (1547-1618)) in Naples. They were both enclosed orders, but one order took simple vows, the other solemn. Ursula patterned the women's communities on the Theatine Fathers, but the Theatine priests had little if anything to do with the order in its earliest years. In 1535 a women's community was established by Contesa Louisa Torelli to assist a new order of men, the Barnabite Fathers, in their apostolate to women. The Oratorian Fathers accepted women into their order in 1575.

Other women did not look to be affiliated with new male orders. They created independent communities built around tried and true customs. The Sisters of St. Marcellina, or Ambrosian Nuns, founded in Italy in 1408; the Benedictine Sisters of the Blessed Sacrament, founded in Switzerland in 1526; the Sisters of St. John of Penance, founded in Spain in 1509; the Sisters of Our Lady of Bethlehem, also founded in Spain in 1525; the Annunciates, founded in France in 1500; and the Sisters of St. Catherine, founded in Germany in 1571 were all new orders that offered little variation on medieval monastic customs; they did offer a more invigorated spirituality. They contributed to an increase in options available to women, and they helped prepare the way, particularly those communities on the Iberian peninsula, for one of the pillars of the Counter Reformation, the Carmelite reform of Teresa of Ávila

Beatas

Women in Spain enjoyed a relatively high degree of equality with men during the Late Middle Ages, and so it should come as no surprise to see women religious there exercise a great deal of authority and occupy positions of highest respect in Reformation society. Actually, Spain was unique in many ways, for it first spearheaded the Catholic Reform and it dominated the Counter Reformation, the official Roman Catholic reform that started with the Council of Trent. Women played a key role in both phases of the reform movement.

As the Catholic Reform was germinating in Spain, women called *beatas* (blessed ones) were participating in the mystical movement that swept over Spain by storm during the 1480s, especially in Castile. Many *beatas* were members of the Franciscan, Dominican, or Augustinian third orders, but the term was used broadly to refer to women who attended daily mass, promoted a highly personalized and often emotional relationship with, God, revered Scripture, wore religious habits, sometimes shaved their heads, did not necessarily owe any superior obedience, took a vow of chastity, and lived a simple existence. Most formed groups, and many lived in houses together, frequently next to parish churches. A few opted for enclosure. Numerous *beaterios* (*beatas* houses) were established in cities such as Seville, Granada, Jaen, Toledo, and Madrid, as well as in smaller towns such as Camarena and Ucles. The number of *beatas* in some cities was as high as 30 percent of all adult women. Baeza, for example, had a total population of twenty thousand in this period and a *beatas* population of two thousand. They came from all walks of life. The church allowed them to preach and to prophesy freely. *Beatas* undertook charitable work wherever they went, and later in the next century when the Spanish church enforced enclosure on nuns, they became the main performers of charitable work among women.

The sphere of influence that these women had was quite considerable. Isabel de la Cruz's lectures in the aristocratic homes of Guadalajara were attended by the laity and the clerical hierarchy, who were duly impressed with her knowledge of Scripture in both Latin and the vernacular. Maria de Cazalla's theology of spiritual abandonment combined with Erasmus' philosophy of Christ was discussed and debated in the University of Alcalá de Henares, then the center of Spain's intellectual life. The prophecies of María de Santa Domingo, the famed *beata* of Piedrahita, were defended and listened to by King Ferdinand and the primate of the Spanish church, Cardinal Ximénes de Cisneros. The women's works were discussed in part because all three of these *beatas* were suspected of heresy. The *beatas*, like many mystics, often flirted with heresy, in this case, the heresy of illuminism (Alumbrado). Isabel de la Cruz called by some the founder of the heresy, taught a radical form of mysticism: the belief that all rational thought must cease to make room for direct communication from God. María de Cazalla eventually cleared herself of charges, and María de Santa Domingo was exonerated before the Inquisition, thanks to the pressure exerted by Cardinal Cisneros. Apparently Cisneros believed that women were important allies in his reform of the Spanish church—he had works of Catherine of Siena and Angela of Foligno (1248-1309) translated and published—which the *beatas* indeed proved to be. They were, however, at certain times and certain places too emotional, given to religious frenzy, too extreme, and perhaps even too bold. *Beatas* were tested and tested by their contemporaries so society could discern the sincere from the unbalanced Even while this was going on, some, like María Vela's confessor, Father Salcedo, were aware that this too could be done to extremes: "In the end," María writes in her autobiography, "he called the Lady Abbess and told her in my presence and in the presence of the Father Friars, that he no longer had the heart to prove my spirit and no longer had the mind to torture me any more."[16] Still, over the course of the Catholic Reform and well into the Counter Reformation the contributions of women mystics to the health of the Spanish church cannot be denied. It is within this atmosphere that Carmelites such as Teresa of Ávila, Ann of St. Barthlomew, María of St. Joseph, and Ann of Jesus were able to thrive.

The Carmelite Reform: Teresa of Ávila

Few women, if any, have had more influence or enjoyed more popularity in the West than Teresa of Ávila (1515-1582). Born into a large and pious family at Ávila in Castile, she was immersed right from birth in the romantic, Catholic, mystical world of the Spanish Golden Age. After a childhood filled with fanciful diversions, such as running away to be martyred by the Moors, building stone hermitages, and writing romances, Teresa was sent at age fifteen, a year after her mother died, to a Augustinian monastery to be educated. There she was weaned away from her more frivolous side and urged to develop her more serious, intellectual nature. A year and a half later, in 1536, a serious illness caused her to be sent home, and there she decided to enter the Carmelite Monastery of the Incarnation. This decision was not based on a full understanding of what such a life would entail: "I had a close friend in another convent and this made me decide that, if I was to be a nun, it should be nowhere but in the house where she was. . . . I began to fear that, if I had died of my illness, I should have gone to hell; and although I could not even then make up my mind to take the habit, I saw that the religious state was the best and safest, and so, gradually, I decided to make myself enter it. . . ."[17] Soon after she entered the monastery, Teresa's illness (perhaps malaria or a nervous disorder) forced her home again, and it took three years for her to recover and return to the monastery. Around 1554 she was given Augustine's *Confessions*, and this precipitated her definitive conversion to the religious life. Teresa began her search for the perfect contemplative environment.

During the next six years Teresa of Jesus (her religious name) experienced raptures and intellectual visions while she and her monastery grew famous throughout the region. The Incarnation was a somewhat typical religious community for its day. It was by no means decadent, but it was as lax as all other monasteries in Castile in matters relating to separation from the world. "Since they had taken no vows of enclosure,"[18] there was very little active or passive enclosure maintained. Visitors could and did come at all hours to the monastery's parlor to converse with the nuns, who in turn behaved as worldly as the visitors did. Much of this occurred because of the dire economic straits most monasteries found themselves in; benefactors who brought the women sustenance expected to be entertained in parlors out of gratitude. Even with such benefactors, many monasteries like the Incarnation could not make ends meet. "Because it was very poor, we nuns often left it for other places where we could live decently and keep our vows."[19]

Teresa's mystical life deepened despite these distractions, and as Spain itself cried out for something deeper, something more spiritually meaningful, a desire to found a new, more austere monastery grew inside her. "One day, after Communion, the Lord earnestly commanded me to pursue this aim with all my strength. He made me great promises; that the house would not fail to be established, that great service would be done Him there, that its name should be St. Joseph's."[20] In August 1562, after one failed attempt in 1560, this desire was actualized with the foundation of the Monastery of St. Joseph in Ávila. This is also the year Teresa finished the first draft of her autobiography, which when finished in 1566 or 1567 deserved a place of honor right next to Augustine's *Confessions*, perhaps the greatest autobiography in world literature. Teresa's position as a major writer in the Spanish Golden Age and the love and esteem generations upon generations have bestowed on her up to our own day are in large part due to this masterpiece. It is impossible to read her *Life* and not be aware of her genius, her incomparable understanding of the human psyche, her down-to-earth common sense, her literary mastery, and her spiritual purity.

The Monastery of St. Joseph was poorly received by the townspeople, who "all agreed that this new convent must on no account be sanctioned"[21] because they worried about how yet another community could be supported. "Once we began to recite the Office in our convent, the people began to be very devoted to the place. More nuns were received, and the Lord began to move those who had persecuted us most to show us favour and give us alms."[22] The women's high standards of behavior eventually won over their opponents. "True, the Rule is rather strict; meat is never eaten except in cases of necessity, there is an eight months' fast, and there are other ascetic practices, as can be seen from the Primitive Rule."[23] The women were strictly contemplative and enclosed, observed near-perpetual silence and abstinence from meat, and practiced extreme poverty. When they wore sandals instead of shoes they gained the name Discalced Carmelites. By 1567 Teresa was planning a second foundation in Medina del Campo. While finalizing the details in that town she met a newly ordained priest, John de Yepes y Alvarez, known to us as John of the Cross. Even though the Medina del Campo house was only Teresa's second foundation, she was already considering how she could extend her reform of the Carmelite Order into the male branch. After persuading John to spearhead her reform, she invited him in 1568 to visit the Valladolid monastery, already her fourth foundation, for a few months so he could familiarize himself with the women's observances. After thus receiving Teresa's training, John proceeded to establish a monastery for friars in a farmhouse in Duruelo, recently donated to Teresa. By 1570 Teresa had helped the men establish themselves at Pastrana near the University of Alcalá, where they also founded a house of studies.

Teresa's desire to reform the friars did not interfere with her activity on behalf of the women. Foundations in Malaga, Toledo, Pastrana, and Salamanca were completed before 1571, when she was called back to her mother house at the Incarnation. Poverty had reduced the women practically to nonobservance of monastic life, and Teresa had been sent for to rescue them. She petitioned John of the Cross to come and serve as the monastery's confessor, and by October 1574 the Monastery of the Incarnation was a Discalced Carmelite community. John was also Teresa's confessor during this period, and under his spiritual direction she attained her highest mystical state. He in turn was as deeply affected by their mutual spiritual relationship as she and began his masterpieces in mystical literature during this period.

The rest of Teresa's life was spent in a flurry of activity and, paradoxically, in peaceful contemplation. Her activity resulted in the foundation of seventeen houses for women and four for men; her contemplation brought forth the greatest of her mystical writings, *The Interior Castle*. After her death in 1582 her reform spread to Italy (1592), France (1604), Belgium (1607), and gradually to the rest of Europe and the New World. Her role in the formation of Counter Reformation culture and of Post-Tridentine (after the Council of Trent) Catholicism is unmatched; the only other contender for such a claim is Ignatius Loyola (1491-1556), founder of the Jesuits. Teresa's contribution to world literature is acknowledged by all, and her theology earned her the distinction of being named a Doctor of the Church, one of only two women (Catherine of Siena is the other) who have been given that prestigious title.

In a book on women religious, however, it is appropriate that we single out one of her numerous contributions for special note. In an age in which women were increasingly drawn to the active apostolate, Teresa reminded her contemporaries that the contemplative fulfilled as important a function for society as did the social worker.

The standard bearer is not a combatant, yet none the less he is exposed to great danger, and inwardly must suffer more than anyone, for he cannot defend himself, as he is carrying the standard which he must not allow to leave his hands, even if he is cut to pieces. Just so contemplatives have to bear aloft the standard of humility and must suffer all the blows which are aimed at them, without striking any themselves. Their duty is to suffer as Christ did, to raise the Cross high, not allow it to leave their hands, whatever the perils in which they find themselves. . . . Let the contemplative consider what he is doing; for, if he lets the standard fall, the battle will be lost.[24]

Teresa's defense of contemplative women religious did not mean that she had no appreciation for active women religious. In fact, her own activity serves as an example for women attracted to both the contemplative life and the active life.

While I was wondering if the people were right who disapproved of my going out to make foundations and if I should better do to occupy myself continually in prayer, I heard these words: "For as long as life lasts, there is no gain to be had in striving to have greater fruition in Me, but only in doing My will." It had seemed to me that, considering what St. Paul says about women keeping at home (I have recently been reminded of this and I had already heard of it), this might be God's will. He said to me: "Tell them they are not to be guided by one part of the Scripture alone, but to look at others; ask them if they suppose they will be able to tie My hands."[25]

Finally, Teresa defended the work of all women, be they active women religious, contemplative women religious, or laywomen.

For when Thou wert in the world, Lord, Thou didst not despise women, but didst always help them and show them great compassion. Thou didst find more faith and no less love in them than in men. . . . Thou art a righteous Judge, not like the judges in the world, who, being after all, men and sons of Adam, refuse to consider any women's virtue as above suspicion. . . . [B]ut, when I see what the times are like, I feel it is not right to repel spirits which are virtuous and brave, even though they be spirits of women.[26]

8

The Transition into
the Modern Age

If we follow Teresa's Carmelite reform into France in 1604, we find
ourselves in the epicenter of developments in Counter Reformation
women's religious communities. Teresa's fame was international even
while she lived, and her spirit continued to inspire women's reform activity
well into the next century. The women whom she trained for religious life
became the means by which the Carmelites spread throughout Europe.
Two in particular, Ann of St. Bartholomew (1549-1626), Teresa's personal
assistant, and Ann of Jesus (d. 1621), were accomplished women leaders
in their own right, as they were to prove when a French delegation headed
by the future cardinal Pierre de Bérulle (1575-1629) went to Spain to invite
them to establish a house in Paris.

It was Barbe Avrillot (1566-1618), wife of Pierre Acarie, who was
responsible for the delegation. Madame Acarie, perhaps the most influential person in early seventeenth century Catholic France and head of a
household that became the core of what we today call the French School,
believed herself to be directly inspired by Teresa to establish a Carmelite
house in France. She turned to her circle of clergy for advice and aid, a
circle that included Bérulle, Francis de Sales, and Beaucousin, and got
them to obtain the necessary permission for such an establishment. While
she waited for their tasks to be completed, Madame Acarie formed the
Congregation of St. Genevieve in her home as a preliminary step for
women who desired eventual entrance into the Carmelite community.
Finally, in 1605, the Parisian Monastery of the Incarnation was opened.

Bérulle insisted that Ann of St. Bartholomew be one of the women to head the French house, but he may have regretted his choice later when the two locked horns over who was in charge. Ann was a woman to be reckoned with, as her tale of one of their many encounters reveals:

> And for a whole hour he [Bérulle] was disputing points in the constitution and the Rule about some things he wanted to change. I contradicted him, and he said he knew these things quite as well as I. I told him that was not so; that he must be great in book-learning, but that he had no experience, as I did, of matters concerning the Order, and that I would never agree to it. And he told me that Spain had one way but France had quite another. I said that the Rule and the constitution must always be one and the same, both here and there, and I would not agree.[1]

Ann and the Spanish women ultimately were victorious in this battle of spirits, for it was their Teresian spirituality that dominated not only the Carmelite houses but the clergy who directed them. Their spirituality in fact permeated the whole of the French School and strongly influenced most French women founders of other religious communities.

RESPONSES TO THE DEMANDS OF THE DAY

The Visitandines: Jane Frances de Chantal

Chief among the latter was a woman named Jane Frances Frémyot de Chantal (1572-1641). She was the inspiring genius behind the foundation and spread of the Visitation Order, an order that was one of the last major active orders forced to become enclosed. At age twenty, Jane married Christopher, baron of Rabutin-Chantal, and she bore four children before her husband's death in 1601. During the next few years the usual social and family obligations dominated her life; her aging father-in-law and her young children needed constant attention and love. A woman of her social position also was expected to assist the poor in her neighborhood, but Jane so surpassed these expectations that soon her charitable works and her impeccable reputation were known to all throughout the area. One of her most exceptional talents was nursing, which she did for the villagers whenever and wherever she was asked. Her work among the poor and ill was organized, efficient, and systematic. Jane took advantage of these diverse social and family activities and used them to shape a unique spirituality that eventually became the basis of her religious community.

It is at times difficult to ascertain the precise role women like Jane Frances played in the formation of the new seventeenth-century religious orders, for the dominant position given to their confessor-spiritual directors usually overshadows the women themselves in foundation narratives and often reduces the women to instruments used by the men. We have seen this happen before, in the histories of Paula's and Melanie the Elder's monasteries. Just as the stories of their monasteries often are told as if Jerome and Rufinus were the sole founders, so too the foundation stories of the seventeenth-century active orders often is told as if men conceived of these orders independent of the women. One of the more blatant examples of this tendency is the accounts given concerning the foundation of the Canonesses Regular of St. Augustine of the Congregation of Our Lady. The originator and founder of the order is almost inevitably cited as Pierre Fourier, yet Alix le Clerc tells us a different story.

> Then I went to see our good Father for the first time in order to tell him my desires. I remarked that when I pray to God I am always filled with the spirit, which must be believed, to found a new order of girls to do all the good that can be done, and this inspiration pressed with such vehemence that I immediately went to propose this to our good father, asking him to give me permission to do all this; but he would not grant me my wish, showing me the difficulty there would be finding the girls who would be willing to embrace such a new vocation. . . . In less than six weeks or two months three girls came to seek me out one after another: Gaute André, Claude Chauvenal and Jeanne de Louvroir. Since then we wanted to live together and in community. . . . I intended to be like St. Ignatius, who inspired me to educate young girls, who in many cases were like delicate straw. . . . However, this vocation was at first denied. This father did not understand this desire to "gather together the poor delicate straw."[2]

Alix's persistence and success in recruiting women eventually persuaded "the good father," Pierre Fournier, to be her confessor-spiritual director and her group's advocate before the hierarchy, for Alix was well aware of the need she had for such help if she hoped to accomplish her goal. By the seventeenth century a peculiar relationship had been worked out among women, their confessor-spiritual directors, and the hierarchy. It was a relationship in which the confessor-spiritual director exercised authority over the women, but the women decided who their confessor-spiritual director would be. After Ann of St. Bartholomew's fight with Cardinal Bérulle, she lamented that "what most afflicted me was confession, for I had to confess to this man."[3] She convinced the Carmelite Superior General, therefore, not only to transfer her to Antwerp where she could have another confessor-spiritual director, but also to agree to the right of all women to choose: "The Superior General desires that if a confessor does not give comfort, he should be changed."[4] Most clergy willingly agreed the confessor-spiritual directors "must be chosen in good faith," as Jean Surin (1600-1665) says, "and by an entirely free choice, and not by force"[5] because it was to the church's advantage, as well as the women's, to find a way for clergy and women to work together. If the church wished to remain a viable institution it needed to restore peace and unity among believers, to catechize the ignorant, and to provide answers to the new social ills of the day. Women could help meet all three demands, and if the hierarchy approached women through the institution of confession, they could be assured that the women would work within the system. Women, on the other hand, needed access to the power structures of their world, and confessor-spiritual directors gave them that access. Confessor-spiritual directors became the mediators between the women's communities and the hierarchy as the women searched for formal approval and protection and the hierarchy searched for apostolic workers. It was Pierre Fourier who argued before a council, in an effort to get Alix's group approved, that throughout Christian history women have enjoyed the right to engage in apostolic work and even in teaching "in private homes."[6] It was Pierre Fourier, not Alix le Clerc, because Alix would not have had the access to the necessary channels of power, nor would have her request or arguments been taken quite as seriously as a request of confessor-spiritual director.

Placing themselves under obedience to one confessor-spiritual director ultimately gave women an uncommon amount of freedom. In 1604 Jane Frances de Chantal signed a written contract with Francis de Sales in which she vowed total obedience to him as her confessor-spiritual director, while at the same time she cautioned her fellow companions that "we show these confessors due respect, yet we explain to them very frankly our liberty of action,"[7] In other words, the relationship was manipulative. Both the confessor-spiritual directors and the women tried "to manage or utilize skillfully" the relationship, as Webster's dictionary defines manipulation. This worked exceedingly well as long as neither used unfair or insidious ways of controlling one another and as long as both remembered the goal was ultimately spiritual.

Jane Frances de Chantal and Francis de Sales were a premier example of how well the relationship could work if nurtured properly.

From Jane's vow of obedience in 1604 until Francis' death in 1622, the two developed a model spiritual friendship. While it is true that Jane was formally under Francis' direction and not vice versa, it is impossible to read the life of Jane and the theology of Francis without seeing how the former shaped the latter; such mutual influence is common to all truly deep relationships. Jane encouraged, supported, and influenced Francis as much as Francis did Jane. When Francis informed Jane of the plan he had for a new, original religious community for women, it really was little more than the institutionalization into communal form of the life he had seen Jane live for years. It was a life of a middle-age mother who, after her family obligations decreased somewhat, filled her days with mental prayer and apostolic work. This was to be a life of a Visitation nun. The order was developed by the two "as a refuge for girls with disabilities, with disfigurements, or for older women and for widows with grown children."[8] The order's ascetic practices were lightened to accommodate those whose "goal to pursue sanctity and greater spiritual health is impeded or hindered because they lack good physical health."[9] They were not enclosed because their special apostolate as Visitandines was to "go out to visit the poor and the sick,"[10] always remembering, however, that visitation "was added as an additional exercise rooted in the devotion of the founders of this congregation and the needs of their neighborhood rather than as the principal end of the congregation."[11]

Because the Visitandines did not take solemn vows, Jane and Francis hoped the women could continue as an nonenclosed community of women. When the Visitation expanded into Lyons in 1615, this status was challenged. The archbishop of Lyons, Denis-Simon de Marquemont, differed greatly with Jane and Francis over the group's right to exist as a nonenclosed community. "No congregation will ever be established here unless it is enclosed by me,"[12] wrote Marquemont, so if they wanted to stay in Lyons they had to transform themselves into a traditional religious order, complete with enclosure. This they did in 1618, and when Francis de Sales died in 1622 the Visitation was indeed a traditional monastic order with twelve houses that did no visiting.

This is not to say it was business as usual, for the Visitation offered something to society that it greatly needed, a lived spirituality that was accessible to all. Under Jane's guidance the Visitation grew tremendously popular as she adapted Salesian spirituality to the common woman, and in the nineteen years after Francis' death and before her own in 1641, she was personally responsible for the establishment of a phenomenal sixty more houses in France, Italy, and Switzerland.

Daughters of Charity

It was with the confessor-spiritual director chosen by Jane Frances de
Chantal after Francis de Sales' death that the final and lasting breakthrough
was made in the formal acceptance of women's active religious communities.
That man was Vincent de Paul (1581-1660). He became involved with the
Visitandines when Francis de Sales appointed him the ecclesiastical director
of the first Parisian Visitation house in 1619. Six years prior to that
appointment, Vincent de Paul had been hired by Marguerite de Gondi to
tutor her children. Through his employer's connections Vincent became
acquainted with most of Catholic Parisian society, including Jane Frances
and Francis de Sales. The seventeenth-century upper-class French Catholics
these three associated with were a curious group with very set goals: to
accept and to implement the reforms dictated by the Council of Trent, and
to address the social problems of a new age. The first generation of these
Catholics, known as the Saints, flourished in the early decades of the century
under the leadership of Madame Acarie. We have already seen the role she
played in bringing the Discalced Carmelites to France; she and her friends
also were responsible for advocating clerical and episcopal reforms, reforms
that they believed were a prerequisite if the laity were to be properly
educated in religious matters. The second generation of these Catholics gave
birth to men and women *dévotes*, that is, pious members of the laity who were
identified by their extreme religiosity and their practice of social work.
Women *dévotes* believed it was more efficient to create institutions directly
engaged in education if the goal of an informed laity was to be achieved.
Hence we see the foundation of about eighteen new French teaching congregations by 1640.[13]

The women *dévotes* were likewise in the forefront of a movement to
solve the problems of the poor. As alluded to earlier, all European society
was having to come to grips with a growing number of urban poor. The
informal, haphazard charity of monasteries, parishes, and individuals was
no longer adequate for the numbers of poor that filled the cities of Europe.
Gradually all neophyte national states of this early modern period were
forced to address this problem, but, unfortunately, their first responses
often were based on impatience and even on a disdain for the poor. France
was particularly hard-pressed by these problems, while at the same time
it was peculiarly blessed by the presence of hundreds and hundreds of
women determined to temper society's intolerant attitude toward the poor
and ready to organize care of the helpless into efficient institutional forms.
With the indispensable aid of confessor-spiritual directors like Vincent de

Paul, these women did just that. They created religious communities that became the backbone and the workforce of the social services of the era.

Vincent's involvement with the problems of dispensing charity began after he left Marguerite de Gondi's household for a rural parish. There he saw women's efforts to help the poor and the sick often duplicated and thus wasted, because they were not centrally organized. He also witnessed the organization of the Visitandines during his years as their confessor-spiritual director. After quickly realizing how organization of the women's charitable works would eliminate duplication and increase efficiency, he constructed an organizational model that met with such success that it spread throughout the area. Other clergy became involved, and in 1625 they formed a congregation called the Priests of the Mission, dedicated to help promote rural women's apostolic work.

After women marshaled their forces and became organized into confraternities of charity in the countryside, they turned their attention to Paris. Small groups of men and women had been quietly organizing themselves since the turn of the century to address the growing problem of the poor and the sick; the Honorable Ladies, the Assembly of Forty Notables, and the Assembly of Mercy were quite effective associations in the second and third decades of the seventeenth century. By the fourth decade the question of the poor was reaching crisis proportions (in 1629 France issued its national law code, which called for the confinement of all the poor), and the *dévotes* responded to the situation. In 1634 Madame Goussault (d. 1639) organized the Ladies of Charity, a successful and popular society of high-ranking Parisian women dedicated to hospital work and a variety of social services.

Madame Goussault's society was at first highly effective. Some of its first members were women who previously had been associated with the parish charitable organizations of Vincent de Paul, so it is not surprising that Vincent became the spiritual director of the Ladies. One of the Ladies was Louise de Marillac (Mlle de Gras), a determined woman who had a gift for leadership. The Ladies of Charities started experiencing problems around 1629 because they had become "a bit less fervent in the exercise of charity. They often fail to visit the sick on their appointed days because the Treasurer is so good-natured that she has the food cooked for them. Moreover, she and the Superioress have sometimes been satisfied with simply giving money to the sick."[14] Soon few were willing actually to serve the sick and the poor in their homes. Louise de Marillac and a peasant named Marguerite Naseau (1598?-1633) provided a solution. Marguerite had spent years in the countryside teaching girls how to read and serving the poor, but at age thirty-two she had decided to go to Paris to help alleviate the suffering of the poor there. Once in Paris she approached the well-known Vincent de Paul, who in turn directed her to Louise. Before long Louise had worked out a long-term solution, by setting up in her home a novitiate of sorts for the training of lower-class women like Marguerite who would be willing to serve the poor. Louise's group became the core members of a religious community known as the Daughters of Charity, the fruit of a collaboration between Louise and Vincent.

As with Francis de Sales and Jane Frances de Chantal, Vincent was the confessor-spiritual director of the group, and hence its defender, promoter, and advocate in the ecclesiastical and secular world, and Louise the backbone, the practical organizer, implementor, and policymaker of the new order. Their relationship was complementary rather than hierarchical (Vincent stops addressing his letters to Louise as "My dear daughter" in 1629; she becomes "Mademoiselle" and he "Monsieur"), even though Louise always gave the appearance of working under Vincent's commands. In theory, Vincent reserved the right to veto Louise's decisions. In practice, they respected each other's ability to make independent decisions, while at the same time remembering that true partners always submit their decisions to the other for final approval. "I beg you most humbly, Monsieur, to take the trouble to inform me how I should act in this matter," wrote Louise when she saw "that this is the opportune time to work for the establishment of the Confraternity of Charity of the parish of Saint-Etienne." As the letter continues, however, we see she already had an elaborate plan in place, so, she writes, it is not really necessary for Vincent to come up with another one, only to send word "if you want something different from what I propose."[15]

The community was at first secular without vows or enclosure. There was a strong emphasis on reading; in their original *Order of the Day*, three periods were reserved for reading or learning to read.[16] The women, often called the Grey Sisters in a very telling if not deliberately conscious realization of the connection between the Daughters of Charity and the earlier fourteenth-century Franciscan tertiaries, were to "imitate in some way the women and young girls of the Gospel" by working "at their own perfection for the salvation of their families and for the corporal and spiritual assistance of the sick and poor of this city and of the country, whom they shall serve themselves in their parishes and for whom they shall procure the able assistance of the Ladies of Charity in the villages."[17] They were, in other words, like so many other active religious organizations that had been established during the previous century in all aspects except one:

They were the first group of women to function as religious without eventually becoming enclosed.

The process by which they were accepted by the hierarchy and by society as nonenclosed women religious can be traced through the actions of Vincent and Louise: Vincent's circumventing the enclosure that solemn vows entailed by proposing private vows without witnesses; Louise's avoidance of the name society, order, or confraternity, since all communities so designated had been forced to become enclosed; and the blatant reminder to anyone desiring the women's enclosure that such enclosure meant the loss of their social services. This last fact probably had more to do with society's acceptance of the nonenclosed women religious than any other. Canon law, inheritance and feudal law, and the social status of women aside, society in general finally realized that these women were providing an irreplaceable service. They had become so indispensable to society that all other factors faded in comparison.

The other factors, of course, remained obstacles to overcome, but once French society had the will to surmount them it did so with relative ease. Episcopal approval was obtained by bishops treating the new communities not as religious orders but as some kind of diocesan confraternity that they then granted the same privileges as religious orders. Once a community received episcopal approbation, it was easier to obtain *lettres patentes* (royal approval), the next necessary step that conferred on the community legal status before the state. Anne of Austria, the regent during Louis XIV's minority, was especially helpful to women seeking such approval of their communities. Finally, the approval had to be registered by *parlement*. Resistant to do so until the 1660s, *parlement* began changing its attitude as a new generation of *parlementaires*, who in their youth had personally witnessed the usefulness of these teaching and nursing women, and consequently held the communities in high esteem, were in charge. By the end of the decade most resistance had disappeared and *parlement's* registration was freely given to any community that met the minimal standards. Given the independence of the seventeeth-century Gallican church, no one even thought it necessary to obtain formal papal approval.

Rome and the rest of Europe eventually followed suit, but seventeenth-century France was indeed unique. The overwhelming response of French women to the call of the apostolic life was phenomenal, both in sheer numbers[18] and in innovation. The Visitandines and the Daughters of Charity have received the most attention from historians because of their charismatic founders and their role at crucial points in the transition to full acceptance of women's active communities, but they were only two of dozens of new active communities founded throughout France during the post-Tridentine era. Again, the rest of Europe was quick to imitate the French example, and before the end of the seventeeth century literally hundreds of active religious communities had been established throughout the continent. The papacy remained legislatively silent on the issues concerning new active orders until the twentieth century. In December 1900 Pope Leo XIII issued the bull *Conditae a Christo* that basically recognized the situation the women had worked out over the two intervening centuries.

The Nuns of Port-Royal

Before we leave France with its Saints and *dévotes*, we would be remiss if we ignored an institute of women religious that became the center of the most notorious theological and political controversy of the day, the nuns of Port-Royal. Port-Royal-des-Champs was originally a poor, insignificant Cistercian monastery near Versailles until Angelique Arnauld (1592?-1661) decided to reform it. Angelique was placed in the monastery by her powerful parents "to be abbess, July 5, 1602, at the age of only ten years, ten months, by a very great abuse common at the time, when there was no longer practice of discipline in the appointment to benefices," Angelique tells us. "The General of the Order of Cîteaux (who had made me a coadjutrix by Madame Boulehart, Abbess of the House, before I was eight, to gratify my grandfather, . . . and had made me Profess at nine), expressed a desire to bless me at his hands at the age of eleven, which he did."[19] Such blatant disregard for regulations did not bother Angelique at the time, but in 1608 she experienced an inner conversion, and in 1609 she infuriated her family and friends when she insisted that the house maintain full observance of the rule.

Reform came to the monastery, and its fame spread throughout the countryside. Angelique's fame grew also, and soon she wished "only to be hidden"[20] in a quiet monastery. She approached the French Carmelites but found them unattractive. Acquaintance with Jane Frances de Chantal "made me think of the Order of S. Mary, the Visitation,"[21] and to that end Angelique began a correspondence with Jane Frances. Angelique also made Francis de Sales' acquaintance during this time and "communicated to him my desire to leave my charge in order to turn simple Nun,"[22] and begged him to receive her into the Congregation of the Visitation. Francis' death in 1622 ended the discussions, and Angelique's place in history ended up quite differently from that of these early friends.

So successful was her reform that the women eventually outgrew the house, and in 1626 they moved into a larger monastery in Paris. The queen mother became their patron, and the reformed nuns of Port-Royal-de-Paris became religious celebrities. As part of her reform, Angelique wanted to eliminate external interference with the internal workings of the community. To that end she severed ties with the Cistercian Order and placed the monastery under the jurisdiction of the bishop of Langres, Sébastien Zamet. Permission from Rome to do so was granted by making Port-Royal the center of a new religious order, the Institute of the Holy Sacrament. In 1629 it received royal approval, but in 1633 it found itself in the eye of its first theological storm. Bishop Zamet asked Angelique's sister Jeanne to write a pamphlet summarizing the new order's ideals. When Jeanne Arnauld finished her *Prayer Beads of the Holy Sacrament*, it was denounced as heretical. Zamet asked Abbé de Saint-Cyran to defend the writings, and when this was successful, Saint-Cyran was invited to become the Institute's confessor-spiritual director. This ultimately had a deleterious effect, for when Saint-Cyran and Zamet developed a bitter rivalry the women had to choose sides. Angelique renounced Zamet and submitted the Institute to the jurisdiction of the archbishop of Paris. He in turn closed the Institute and moved the women to the outskirts of Paris. Saint-Cyran next antagonized the powerful Cardinal Richelieu, Louis XIII's chief minister (1624-42), and by 1638 Saint-Cyran's enemies, which by this time included most bishops, all Jesuits, and the king himself, had him imprisoned. Even while in prison, though, he remained the director of the Port-Royal women, and when his letters of advice to them were published, they caused a stir. His enemies used these letters to prove his adherence to a popular heresy, Jansenism. Based on too Calvinistic an interpretation of grace, predestination, and free will for most Catholics, the Jansenist heresy had two lives, one that functioned at the highest political levels and one that inspired a pietistic movement among the people.

As the controversy grew Port-Royal increasingly became identified with both its political and pietistic forms. By 1653 Angelique and some of the nuns moved back to their original monastery at Port-Royal-des-Champs, which quickly became the stronghold of all Jansenist activity. The women and the heresy grew in popularity and in their ability to threaten the ruling class, until the young Louis XIV decided to rule in his own right in March 1661. Within a month he addressed the problem of Port-Royal by ordering all churchmen, nuns, and lay schoolteachers (Saint-Cyran had established the Little Schools in 1638 at Port-Royal-des-Champs) to sign a document disavowing Jansenism. He then expelled all women aspiring to become nuns at Port-Royal; and he ordered the arrest of all confessor-spiritual directors of Port-Royal. Angelique Arnauld was spared the final conflict, for she died in May 1661. Some women signed, some signed and then retracted, and others refused to sign. By 1665 only submissive nuns remained at Port-Royal-de-Paris, and all dissenting nuns were housed at Port-Royal-des-Champs, where they were deprived of the sacraments and confessors. Finally, when Clement IX was elected pope in 1667 he acted to end the conflict, and in 1669 the nuns were once more admitted into full reception of the church. When the Jansenists once more became politically burdensome to Louis XIV at the turn of the century, Port-Royal-des-Champs was destroyed. All remaining nuns were dispersed forever by 1711.

English Ladies: The Institute of the Blessed Virgin Mary

Not all religious communities, of course, were as politically powerful as the women at Port-Royal, nor did all communities have as easy a time establishing themselves as the Daughters of Charity did. One of the more unfortunate stories of the period concerns the foundation of the Institute of the Blessed Virgin Mary by Mary Ward (1585-1645). It is a story filled with temporary triumphs and temporary defeats, and, for the person intent upon analyzing the struggles of the active orders in their pursuit of acceptance, with much to ponder.

Born at Mulwith, in Yorkshire, after the Elizabethans decided that Catholics were *personae non gratae*, Mary Ward became immersed in the recusant (English Catholics who refused to attend Anglican services) culture in 1606 when she left England to enter the religious community of the Poor Clares at St. Omer, in Flanders. Within months she realized that this type of religious life was not for her. She returned to England, where a group of women interested in apostolic work formed around her. In 1609 Mary crossed the channel once again, this time with her group to set up a boarding school for recusant young girls, a day school for local girls, and a community house for the women teachers. The enterprise was successful, and soon Mary found herself pressed "by diverse spiritual and learned men that we would take upon us some rule already confirmed." Mary, however, had a rather particular nontraditional idea about the type of community she wished to form and thus was not satisfied with the "several rules procured by our friends both from Italy and France." She judged the rules "not that which God would have done, and the refusal of them caused much persecutions,"[23] which continued until Mary finally identified a rule compatible with her aims. Unfortunately for the fate of the community, Mary decided after she "heard distinctly, not by sound of voice but intellectually understood, these words, 'Take the same of the Society,'"[24] to adopt the rule and constitution of the Jesuits (the common name for members of the Society of Jesus). It was unfortunate because this choice was responsible for most of the opposition the Institute experienced. Mary never intended to establish a female branch of the Jesuits, rather only to engage in the same educational work as they did. To Mary the rule of the Society was a logical choice, for if it helped form a male community suited to fulfill the educational needs of the male members of Catholic society, surely it could do the same for a female community desiring to educate the female members.

"My confessor resisted," Mary noted, and "all the Society opposed."[25] Gradually she converted some opponents into supporters, or at least lowered their opposition enough to get a letter of approval from her friend Bishop Blaise before he died in 1618, and then later, in 1621, when she was appealing to Rome for confirmation, letters of recommendation from Archduchess Isabella, Philip IV, and Emperor Ferdinand II. Mary journeyed to Rome in 1621 to petition Gregory XV personally on behalf of her Institute. She had reason to believe approval would be forthcoming. Her community had greatly increased during its first decade. There were already sixty members by 1616, and by 1621 they had houses in London, Cologne, Trier, and two houses in Liége. Also, during the same decade members of the hierarchy had come to appreciate both the need to teach young girls and the usefulness of women teachers in the struggle for the souls of the next generation. Mary was much encouraged.

Unfortunately, Mary's attraction to the Jesuit model was a problem from the beginning. Not only did she want to adapt the *Rule of St. Ignatius* to a women's society, but, like the Jesuits, she wanted the Institute to have an internal general answerable only to the pope. This would have created mother generals. This radical approach alarmed recusant English clergy, who, first of all, distrusted all things Jesuit, and, second, believed a mother general was a ploy to avoid the clergy's direction. It also alarmed the Jesuits, who, paradoxically, did not want to direct them and feared that the pastoral care of the English Ladies would eventually fall to them. The Jesuit father general Vitelleschi was quite opposed to the Institute from the beginning and even removed a Jesuit priest, John Gerard, from his rectorship in Liége in 1623 because he had aided the English Ladies in their foundations. Mary's submission of a written memorial to the papacy articulating the aims of the Institute, plus her personal diplomacy, temporarily won some support for her cause, but after four meetings with the Congregation of Bishops and Regulars (the board charged with approving new orders), it was apparent that she was not going to receive confirmation. To forestall this final verdict she petitioned at a fifth session for permission to establish a communal house and school in Rome so the cardinals and bishops could judge for themselves the value of the Institute. Permission was granted and the establishments were immediate and huge successes. She followed these with similarly successful schools in Naples (1623) and Perugia (1624).

All this proved to be of no avail because opposition was now united against her and the Institute. A rift had occurred in two of the Institute's houses in Liége and in St. Omer's, which resulted in testimonies against Mary by an ex-superior of the Institute, Mary Allcock. Such internal dissent was used by the Institute's enemies to fan further opposition to the English Ladies. But again, it was society's perception of the women as "Jesuitesses" that was in the end responsible for the Institute's suppression. By 1622 a new papal office, the Congregation of Propaganda, had been formed and charged with reviewing new orders. It was headed by Francis Ingoli, a known antagonist of the Jesuits. He quickly extended his antipathy toward Jesuits to include Mary's "Jesuitesses." In July 1624 Ingoli and the Congregation declared that the women must be enclosed, which in effect meant that the Congregation denied the Institute permission to found and teach in schools. In October Mary met with the new pope, Urban VIII. The audience led to a bond of friendship between the two, but not to confirmation of the order. Consequently Mary modified her request by asking permission to establish the Institute only in those areas where English Catholics had congregated in large numbers: Flanders, Germany, and England proper. She also said she would enforce a membership limit of one hundred.

Still this was to no avail; recusant English clergy and the Congregation of Propaganda were poised to issue the death blow. In April 1628 orders were sent to the papal nuncios of Brussels, Cologne, and Vienna to suppress the Institute in those towns. Before the orders could be implemented, Mary again made her way to Rome (she had left Rome in 1626 at the personal invitation of Electorial Duke Maximilian and Emperor Ferdinand II to establish houses in Munich and Vienna) to plead one more time for the Institute's survival. Ingoli was just as determined not to allow it, and since the Congregation of Propaganda's instructions for suppression of the Institute were still not implemented by the end of 1630, Ingoli persuaded Urban VIII to condemn the Institute formally in a papal bull of suppression. This was done on January 13, 1631. On February 7, unbeknownst to Urban VIII, Ingoli had Mary Ward, now in Munich, imprisoned and "declared a heretic, a schismatic, an obstinate rebel against Holy Church, . . . to [be] deprived of the Holy Sacraments . . . and thrown by orders of Holy Church into the jaws of death."[26] Urban VIII proved to be a true friend, for when word finally reached him of her imprisonment, he ordered her released. Once again Mary Ward traveled to Rome, and this time, by dealing solely with the pope, she had limited success. Urban VIII granted her permission to start over again with a new rule.

At the time of the bull the Institute had ten houses and about three hundred women members. The suppression closed down all houses except in Munich and Rome. Rome became the center of the second Institute, which did indeed thrive. In 1703 the Institute of the Blessed Virgin Mary was finally granted full canonical status as a religious congregation, and in 1903 Mary Ward was formally restored to her claim as founder of the order.

Many aspects of the story of Mary and her Institute are instructive, not the least important being the vast complexities of the day. The Reformation brought to light many pressing problems, and agreement on solutions was rare. New innovative women's communities were not alone in being the objects of attack; innovative men's communities also received abundant criticism. It already has been pointed out that the bulk of criticism against the Institute was precisely due to its identification, right or wrong, with the much-maligned Jesuits. There was also the ever-intense conflict and lack of clarity with lines of authority: the pope, the Congregation of Propaganda, the papal nuncios, the local bishops, the archduke, and the emperor all had their own instructions and opinions about the unofficial order of suppression in 1628, and hence no one, least of all Mary, was sure whether her houses in these cities had to be closed, a situation that was clarified only some two and a half years later. There was, of course, the issue of enclosure and the canonical status of nonenclosed women's religious communities, an issue that has pervaded the narrative found in the last few chapters. With Mary Ward we also come face to face with another complex issue: the hierarchy's misogynistic attitude toward women religious.

Throughout the history of religious life, churchmen's attitudes toward women religious were probably less misogynistic that their attitudes toward any other women's group. Certainly the double standard that permeated all segments of society also tainted religious life, but only rarely did it dominate and never did it completely triumph. Treatment of women religious does not suddenly become extremely misogynistic during this period; what changes is that some women religious challenge it. Teresa of Ávila's writings are filled with gentle and not-so-gentle chidings aimed at prodding the hierarchy into realizing that their attitudes toward women were ultimately depriving them of needed assistance in the salvific work of the church. Some of Teresa's disciples, such as María of St. Joseph, were more direct in their criticism. In her *Book of Recreations*, she argues at length that it is because men "have gloried in holding women to be weak, inconstant, imperfect, and indeed useless and unworthy of any noble undertaking" that "whatever we might say has little strength and is given no credence at all because we are women";[27] and women's help is rejected. By the seventeenth century we find an increasing amount of women's criticisms of the situation, and in this body of literature Mary Ward's remarks stand out as particularly pointed. If the three lectures of hers that were recorded and preserved are at all indicative of the logic and the passion with which she analyzed women's position in the church, then it is no wonder that the hierarchy feared a Mary Ward answerable only to the pope. The occasion for her celebrated "Verity speech" was to repudiate a remark a priest made that the goals of the Institute would never be achieved because "when all is done, they are but women."[28] Her anger and impatience at such a mentality is evident throughout the speech. For Mary, sanctity comes to all who have "a will to do well, which women may have as well as men. There is no such difference between men and women that women may not do great things," and women "in time to come will do much" if they take control of their own destiny.

> Are we so inferior to other creatures that they should term us "but women?" For what think you of this word, "but women?" but as if we were in all things inferior to some other creature which I suppose to be man! Which I dare to be bold to say is a lie.[29]

But we also see another element in Mary's speech that is consistent with the actions of so many women religious trying to break new ground during the seventeenth century: awareness that truth was on her side. Men like the priest who expressed such misogynistic attitudes "may have much knowledge and perhaps he hath all other knowledge," but Mary knows this much: "I have only this knowledge and light of this only verity, by which, perhaps, I must be saved. Therefore I must and will ever stand for this verity, that women may be perfect, and that fervour must not necessarily decay because we are women."[30]

> I would to God that all men understood this verity, that women if they will be perfect, and if they would not make us believe we can do nothing, and that we are but women, we might do great matters.[31]

Conclusion

Mary Ward's belief that women "might do great matters" proved to be factual. In the next three centuries women religious made many critical contributions to society: They played major roles in the organization of social services, in the institutionalization of health care facilities, in the development of the professional nurse, in the colonization of the non-Western world, and in the creation of modern pedagogy. In the United States they administered and staffed the world's largest and most successful private education system. But this is not the appropriate place to discuss their achievements; they deserve their own volume.

What is appropriate are some parting remarks as we come to the end of our narrative. We have met many of the individuals who dominated the history of women's religious societies, and we have reviewed a variety of types of life and communities that these women established in their pursuit of an intense religious experience. The quantity and quality of their creativity is impressive, as is their determination to achieve the goals they set for themselves. Often these goals were not realized because of opposition from men religious, but in a surprisingly high number of instances the women invented ways to overcome the obstacles. In part because of this occasional conflict between women and men religious, the history of women religious must be told separate from the men's if we hope to comprehend the women's point of view.

More important, it is evident by now that the history of women religious is not an echo or mirror image of that of men religious. While they shared many, many characteristics and goals, their histories are still distinct from and independent of each other. The history of women religious cannot be told properly by adding a chapter at the end of a history of men religious. It first must be told in its own context, at length, and on its own terms. Only then will the historian be able to synthesize the two histories into a definitive history of religious societies.

Even though the number of women religious was always a small percentage of the total female population, their historical significance is far greater than their numbers alone would indicate. Much has been written of late about how essential the option of religious life was for women and for their ability to control their own lives. This thesis has been demonstrated time and again in this narrative. Religious life offered women an alternative to marriage, regardless of the wishes of parents (Christina of Markyate), and an alternative to bearing children (Melanie the Younger). It offered them a place to function on their own, away from familiar control (Angela Arnauld). Very frequently it provided them with a means to become educated (Lioba) and even sometimes with the means to develop their creative genius in the arts (Hildegard of Bingen) and literature (Hrotsvith). It reserved the only positions of authority society designated exclusively for women (the abbess). In its asexual theology of sanctity women were equal to men (Paula). On occasion it provided a platform for political power (Hilda of Whitby). Often it became the means for women to adapt to new social conditions (Mary of Oignes) and to solve new social problems (Loiuse de Marillac). Because it provided women with all these opportunities, religious life played a more significant role in women's history than it does in men's history. Men had other options; women did not.

To truly grasp the historical significance of religious life for women, however, we must delve a bit deeper into their own understanding of what it offered them. While religious life did indeed offer women alternatives to marriage, an education, independence, and so forth, I know of no primary source where women explicitly state any of those reasons as why they pursued religious life. In every instance they tell us their reason was religiously motivated. They wanted to become saints. They wanted to become one with Christ in heaven. We rarely talk like that anymore, and often do not know what to do with such statements. Yet it is quite easy to translate "desire for sanctity and heaven" into modern parlance. To attain sanctity one has to realize one's potential, to use a common twentieth-century phrase. A saint has to eliminate all weaknesses, overcome all limitations, and strengthen all virtues. She must remove all barriers that make her imperfect—that hinder her from actualizing her full potential as be. The most one can be is a complete human being, and a human being — a creature — is complete only when she is united with her creator. Thus the reality behind the desire for heaven and the desire to realize one's potential are one and the same. Ancient, medieval, and early modern women became women religious because they saw this as a way of realizing their potential: a way to get to heaven. This is perhaps the greatest achievement of women religious. They used religious life to perfect their humanness. They immersed themselves in monasticism, they became anchorites, they developed communities to care for the sick, and they established houses for working single women, all because they believed that to do so was to become Christ-like. In their world, to be one with Christ was to be as fully human as possible. They became women religious to become saints, and along the way they became models of human behavior who had tremendous influence on their contemporaries.

Notes

Abbreviations Used in the Notes

AASS   *Acta Sanctorum,* 2nd ed. Edited by Jean Carnandlt. Paris: V. Palme, 1863.

Book   *The Book of Paradise being the Histories and Sayings of the Monks and Ascetics of the Egyptian Desert by Palladius, Hieronymus, and Others. The Syrian Texts, According to the Recension of Anan-Isho of Beth Abb.* Edited and translated by E. A. Wallis Budge. London: Printed for Lady Meux by W. Drugulen, 1904.

MGH   *Monumenta Germaniae Historica. Scriptores.* Edited by G. H. Pertz et al. Hanover, 1826-1913.

NPNF   *Nicene and Post Nicene Fathers of the Christian Church.* Edited by Phillip Schaff and Henry Wace. 2nd series. New York: The Christian Literature Co., 1893.

PL   *Patrolgia curcus completus: Series Latina.* Edited by J.-P. Migne. Paris, 1844-1864.

Preface

1. Athanasius, *The Life of St. Anthony, 1,* in Budge, *Book,* 1:9-10.
2. Mary Martin McLaughlin, "Looking for Medieval Women," *Medieval Prosopography* 8 (Spring 1987), 61-91.

Chapter 1:
The Beginning

1. Hieronymus, *The Book of Paradise,* in Budge, *Book,* 1:577.
2. Palladius, *The Paradise, or the Book of the Triumphs of the Holy Fathers,* in ibid., 1:220.
3. *Palladius: The Lausaic History,* trans. Robert T. Meyer (New York: Newman Press, 1964), foreword:4.

4. See Palladius, *Paradise*, in Budge, *Book*, 1:337-338, and A. L. Fisher, "Women and Gender in Palladius' *Lausaic History*," *Studia Monastica* 33 (1991), 24-26.

5. Palladius, *Paradise*, in Budge, *Book*, I:229.

6. Gregory of Nyssa, *The Life of St. Macrina*, trans. W. K. Lowther Clarke (London: Society for Promoting Christian Knowledge, 1916), p. 28.

7. Jerome, quoted in *The History of Paula*, trans. N. F. Lagrange, in Mary E. Herbert, *Wives and Mothers in Olden Times*, 2nd ed. (London: A. Bentley and Son, 1885), p. 286.

8. Jerome, Letter 127, in *Select Letters of St. Jerome*, trans. F. A. Wright (repr., Cambridge, MA: Harvard University Press, 1954), pp. 448-449.

9. Jerome, Letter 45, in ibid., pp. 188-189.

10. Jerome, Letter 127, in ibid., pp. 454-455.

11. Ibid., pp. 459-461.

12. Paulinas of Nola, Ep. 8, in *Corpus Scriptorum Ecclesiasticorum Latinorum*, ed. Wilhelm A. Hartel (Vidobonae: F. Tempsky, 1894), 29:253-254.

13. Meyer, *Palladius: Lausiac History*, 46.6.

14. Ibid., 54.1-2.

15. Ibid., 55.3.

16. Jerome, Letter 127, in Wright, trans., *Letters of St. Jerome*, pp. 452-453.

17. Jerome, Letter 29, in Jean Steinmann, *Saint Jerome and His Times*, trans. Ronald Matthews (Notre Dame: Fides Publishers, 1959), p. 144.

18. Jerome, Letter 39, 1, in Schaff and Wace, *NPNF*, 6:49

19. *The Life of Melanie the Younger*, trans. Elizabeth A. Clark (Lewiston, NY: Edwin Mellon Press, 1984), p. 6.

20. Ibid., p. 9.

21. Ibid., p. 26.

22. Ibid., p. 40.

23. Ibid., p. 41.

24. Ibid., p. 47.

25. Ibid., p. 45.

26. Ibid., p. 43.

27. Ibid., p. 44.

28. Ibid., p. 54.

29. Ibid., p. 58.

30. Gregory, *Life of St. Macrina*, pp. 27-51. "Philosophy" in fourth-century literature often means Christianity.

31. Ibid., pp. 34-36.

32. Ibid., p. 71.

33. C. H. Lawrence, *Medieval Monasticism* (London: Longman and Co., 1984), p. 9.

34. Clark, *Melanie the Younger*, p. 20.

35. *The Ecclesiastical History of Sozomen*, 8:9 in Schaff and Wace, *NPNF*, 2:405.

36. *The Life of St. Olympias*, trans. in Herbert, *Wives*, p. 431.

37. Meyer, *Palladius: Lausiac History*, 56.2.

Chapter 2:
Women Religious in the Early Medieval West

1. *Egeria's Travels,* trans. John Wilkinson (London: S.P.C.K., 1971), 3:8 and 5:8-9.
2. *Gregory of Tours: Life of the Fathers,* 2nd ed., trans. Edward James (Liverpool: Liverpool University Press, 1991) 1:6.
3. Patrick, *Letter to Coroticus,* 12, in *St. Patrick. His Writings and Muirchu's Life,* ed. and trans. A. B. E. Hood (London: Phillimore, 1978), p. 57.
4. Patrick, *Dedication,* 42, in ibid., p. 50.
5. *Vita S. Brigidae,* prologue, quoted in John Ryan, *Irish Monasticism: Origins and Development* (repr.; Dublin: Irish Academic Press, 1986), p. 135.
6. Cogitosus, quoted in (Sr.) Mary P. Heinrich, *The Canonesses and Education in the Early Middle Ages* (Washington, D.C.: The Catholic University of America Press, 1924), p. 90.
7. *Vita* in *AASS,* Jan. 15, 1:1062-1068
8. *Vita sancti Caesarii,* in *AASS,* Aug. 27, 6:50-54.
9. The *Rule for Nuns,* 48, in Mary McCarthy, *The Rule for Nuns of St. Caesarius of Arles: A Translation with a Critical Introduction* (Washington, D.C.: The Catholic University of America Press, 1960), p. 187.
10. Ibid., 1, p. 170.
11. *Historia monachorum,* 17, quoted in Adalbert de Vogue, "Caesarius of Arles and the Origin of the Enclosure of Nuns," *Word and Spirit* 11 (1989), 19.
12. Jerome, Letter 108, 20, in Schaff and Wace, *NPNF,* 6:206.
13. *Vita Patrum Iurensium,* 26, quoted in de Vogue, "Enclosure," 21-22.
14. *Rule for Nuns,* 5, in McCarthy, *Rule of St. Caesarius,* p. 172.
15. Ibid., 67, p. 196.
16. *The Life of the Holy Radegund by Venantius Fortunatus,* 4, in *Sainted Women in the Dark Ages,* ed. and trans. JoAnn McNamara and John Halborg, with E. G. Whatley (Durham, NC: Duke University Press, 1992), p. 72.
17. Ibid., 19, p. 78.
18. *The Life of Radegund by Baudonivia,* 2, 5, in ibid., p. 89.
19. Ibid., 10, p. 93.
20. *History of the Franks by Gregory, Bishop of Tours,* trans. Ernest Brehaut (New York: Columbia University Press, 1916), 10:15.
21. Ibid., 10:15-16.
22. Jane T. Schulenburg, "Women's Monastic Communities, 500-1100," *Signs* 14, no. 2 (1989), 266. In the sixth century, 9.8 percent of all new foundations were for women; in the eighth century, 12.4 percent were for women.
23. Bede, *A History of the English Church and People,* trans. Leo Sherley-Price, rev. R. E. Lantham (repr.; Harmondsworth: Penguin Books, 1986), 3:8.
24. Ibid.
25. *Vita sanctae Bathildis,* 7-9, in McNamara and Halborg, eds., *Sainted Women,* pp. 271-273.
26. *Vita Bertilae abbatissae Calensis,* 5, in ibid., p. 285.

27. Bede, *English Church*, 4:23.
28. Ibid.
29. Lioba to Boniface, Letter 21 (29), in *Letters of Saint Boniface*, trans. Ephraim Emerton (New York: Octagon Books, 1973), p. 60.
30. *The Life of Leoba by Rudolf, Monk of Fulda*, in *Anglo-Saxon Missionaries in Germany*, ed. and trans. C. H. Talbot (New York: Sheed and Ward, 1954), p. 222.
31. Ibid., p. 215.
32. Letter 29 (96), in *Letters of Boniface*, p. 173.

Chapter 3:
Restriction and Revival

1. Jane Tibbets Schulenburg, "Women's Monastic Communities, 500-1100," *Signs* 14, no. 2 (1989), 266.
2. Ibid., 276.
3. Aethelwold, *Regularis Concordia*, 3, trans. Thomas Symons. (London: Thomas Nelson and Sons Ltd. 1953), p. 2.
4. Emile Lesne, *Histoire de la propriété ecclésiastique en France* (Paris-Lille: H. Champion-R. Giard, 1910-1943), 6:208.
5. *AASS*, Mar. 22, 3:609.
6. Agius, *Vita et Obitus Hathumodae*, ch. 5, trans. in Lina Eckenstein, *Women under Monasticism* (reissue; New York: Russell and Russell, 1963), pp. 155-156.
7. Agius, ch. 9, trans. in ibid., p. 156.
8. Hrotsvith, *Opera*, trans. in ibid., p.169.
9. Joachim Wollasch, "A Clunaic Necrology from the Time of Abbot Hugh," in *Clunaic Monasticism in the Central Middle Ages*, ed. Noreen Hunt (Hamden, CT: Archon Books, 1971), p. 181.
10. *PL* 189, pp. 889-91.
11. Rome also may have been the destiny of these migrations; St. Mary's in Campo Martes was one such women's monastery.
12. Cf. Francesca M. Steele, *Anchoresses of the West* (London: Sands and Co., 1903).
13. As, for example, Bertha, Monegondes, and Bertilie. See Chapter 2.
14. See *PL* 171, 1481-82; *PL* 157, 181-83.
15. Cf. Sharon K. Elkins, *Holy Women of Twelfth Century England* (Chapel Hill: University of North Carolina Press, 1988), pp. 22-40.
16. *The Life of Christina of Markyate: A Twelfth Century Recluse*, ed. and trans. Charles H. Talbot (Oxford: Clarendon Press, 1959), pp. 73-75.
17. Ibid., p. 103.
18. "Deinde secundum genus es anachoritarum, id est eremitarum," *RB 1980. The Rule of St. Benedict in Latin and English with Notes*, ed. Timothy Fry (Collegeville, MN: The Liturgical Press, 1981), p. 168.

19. Aelred of Rievaulx, *Rule of Life for a Recluse*, 1:2-3, in *The Works of Aelred of Rievaulx*, vol. 1: *Treatises. The Pastoral Prayer*, trans. M. P. Macpherson (Spencer, MA: Cistercian Publications, 1971), pp. 46-47.

20. Ibid., 1:4, pp. 49-50.

Chapter 4:
The Fruits of the Monastic Revival

1. *PL* 162, 1051.

2. *PL* 162, 1051 and 1055.

3. *PL* 162, 1083-1084 .

4. "Historia calamitatum," in *The Letters of Abelard and Heloise*, trans. Betty Radice (repr.; Harmondsworth: Penguin Books, 1984), p. 69.

5. Letter 3, in ibid., p. 134.

6. Letter 7, in ibid., p. 183.

7. Ibid., p. 212.

8. Ibid., p. 197.

9. Ibid., p. 200.

10. Ibid., p. 202.

11. Ibid., p. 201.

12. Ibid., p. 213.

13. Ibid., p. 212.

14. Petrus Abaelardus, "Excerpta e Regulis Paracletensis Monasterii: Epistolae, Petri Abaelardi et Heloisae," in *Petrus Abaelardus Opera*, ed. Victor Cousin (Paris: A. Durand, 1849; repr. Hildesheim, NY: Georg Olms Verlag, 1970), 1:214.

15. "Historia calamitatum" in Radice, *Letters*, p. 97.

16. Letter 115, in ibid., p. 278.

17. *MGH, SS*, 7:695.

18. E. L. Hugo, *Annals Praemonstratenses*, ii, 147, trans. in Richard W. Southern, *Western Society and the Church in the Middle Ages* (London: Penguin Books, 1970), p. 314.

19. L. Horstkötter, "Die Prämonstratenser und ihre Klöster am Niederrhein und in Westfalen," in *Norbert von Xanten*, ed. Kasper Elm (Cologne: Weinand, 1984), pp. 264-265.

20. "Institutiones de laicis sororibus," I, in William Dugdale, *A History of Abbies in Latin, New Edition*, ed. J. Caley, H. Ellis, and B. Bandinel (London: Harding, 1830), 6. 2. 87.

21. *Vita S. Gilbert Confessoris*, "Vocatio sororum laicarum," in ibid., 6. 2. 10.

22. "Institutiones de laicis sororibus," in ibid., 6. 2. 86-88.

23. Ibid., 6. 2. 72.

24. Brian Golding, "The Distortion of a Dream: Transformation and Mutation of the Rule of St. Gilbert," *Word and Spirit* 11 (1989), 60-78.

25. See Janet I. Summers, "The Violent Shall Take It by Force: The First Century of Cistercian Nuns, 1125-1228," Ph.D. diss., University of Chicago, 1986.

26. Quoted in ibid., p. 174.

27. Statute 1191.7, trans. in M. Connor, "The First Cistercian Nuns and Renewal Today," *Cistercian Studies* 5 (1989), 137.

Chapter 5:
The Appeal of the *Vita Apostolica*

1. *PL* 195, 30-31.

2. Thomas of Celano, *First Life of St. Francis of Assisi. Writings and Early Biographies*, ed. Marion A. Habig (Chicago: Franciscan Herald Press, 1983), 9:22.

3. Thomas de Celano, *Legenda sanctae Clarae virginis: tratta dal ms. 338 della Bibbl. communale di Assisi*, ed. F. Pennachi (Assisi: Metastasio, 1910), p. 6.

4. Ibid., p. 10.

5. Ibid.

6. *Lettres de Jacques de Vitry*, ed. R. B. C. Huygens (Leiden: E. J. Brill, 1960), pp. 75-76.

7. S. Clara, *Testamentum*, in *Claire d'Assise Écrits. Introduction, texte latin, traduction notes et index*, ed. M. F. Becker, J. F. Godet, and T. Matura (Paris: Les Éditions du Cerf, 1985), 27-29. This is repeated in *Regula*, in ibid., 6:3.

8. *Testamentum*, in ibid., 27-29.

9. "Privilegium paupertatis (1216)," in *ibid.*, p. 196, 198.

10. Thomas de Celano, *Legenda*, p. 14.

11. Ibid.

12. "Privilegium paupertatis (1228)," in *Écrits*, p. 200..

13. Thomas de Celano, *Legenda*, p. 24.

14. Clara, *Testamentum*, in *Écrits*, pp. 19-23.

15. "Periculoso ac detestabili," *Sextus liber Decretalium*, 1.2, tit. 15, ed. A. Friedberg, *Corpus iuris canonici*, 2, (Lipsiae: Berndardus Tauchnitz, 1922), 1053-1054.

16. Bernard Gui, *Monumenta Ordinis Praedicatorum Historica*, trans. in *Early Dominicans: Selected Writings*, ed. Simon Tugwell (New York: Paulist Press, 1982), p. 389.

17. Ibid., p. 390.

18. *The Chronicles of St. Agnes' Monastery*, in ibid., p. 395.

19. Ibid., pp. 395-396.

20. Ibid., p. 399.

21. Joseph Greven, "Der Ursprung des Beginenwesens," *Historisches Jahrbuch* 35 (1914), 47.

22. *AASS*, June 23, 5:568.

23. Gertrude the Great, trans. in *Medieval Women's Visionary Literature*, ed. Elizabeth A. Petroff (New York: Oxford University Press, 1986), p. 209.

Chapter 6:
The Visionary Late Medieval Period

1. Bonaventura, *Libellus Apologeticus* in *Opera omnia*, ed. A. C. Peltier (Paris: L. Vives 1864-1871), 14:534.

2. Girolamo Tiraboschi, *Vetera Humiliatorum Monumenta Annotationibus* (Milan: J. Galeatius, 1766-1768), 2: 133-134.

3. *Catherine of Siena: the Dialogue,* trans. Suzanne Noffke (New York: Paulist Press, 1980), prol. 1. p. 26.

4. Angela *of Foligno. The Complete Works,* trans. Paul Lachance (New York: Paulist Press, 1993), p. 127.

5. Ibid., p. 139.

6. Salome Sticken, *A Way of Life for Sisters,* in *Devoto Moderna: Basic Writings,* trans. John van Engen (New York: Paulist Press, 1988), p. 181.

7. Ibid., p. 182.

8. David Knowles, *The Religious Orders of England* (Cambridge: University of Cambridge Press: 1959) 3: 463.

9. Dayton Phillips, "Beguines in Medieval Strasburg: A Study of the Social Aspects of the Beguine Life," Ph.D. diss., Stanford University, 194 1, p. 19.

10. "Second Letter to Clara Gambacorta from Saint Catherine of Siena" trans. in Mary E. Murphy, "Blessed Clara Gambacorta," Ph.D. diss., University of Fribourg, 1928, p. 171.

11. Bulle, no. 1004, "Devotionis tuae," in *St. Colette and Her Reform,* trans. Conor Macquire, ed. G. O'Neill (Londo n: Sands and Co.), 1923), app. 2, pp. 338-340.

12. "First Letter of the Very Rev. Father William of Casal to Coletta, : trans. in *First Rule of Saint Clare and the Constitution of Saint Coletta* (London: Thomas Richardson, 1875), pp. 96- 97.

13. *Solet annuere,* Bull of Pius II, in ibid., pp. 114-115.

14. Ibid., p. 107.

15. Ibid., pp. 108- 109.

16. *The Life of Blessed Birgitta by Prior Peter and Master Peter,* 48, in *Birgitta of Sweden: Life and Sleceted Revelations,* ed. M. T. Harris, trans. A. R. Kezel (New York: Paulist Press, 1990), pp. 85- 86.

17. *Regula Salvatoris,* 29: 283-286, in *Sancta Birgitta Opera Minora I: Regula Salvatoris,* ed. Sten Eklund (Stockholm: Almqvist and Wiksell International, 1975), pp. 134- 135.

18. *Life of Blessed Birgitta,* 49, in Harris, ed., *Birgitta of Sweden,* p. 86.

19. *Extrauagancium 44,* 1-7, in *Den Heliga Birgittas, Reuelaciones. Extrauagantes,* ed. Lennart Hollman (Uppsala: Almqvist and Wiksells Boktryckeri, 1956), pp. 160-161.

20. *The Fourth Book of Revelations,* 138, in Joan Bechtold, "St. Birgitta: The Disjunction Between Women and Ecclesiastical Male Power" in *Equally in God's Image,* ed. Julia B. Holloway, C. Wright, and J. Bechtold (New York: Peter Lang Publishers, 1990), p. 99.

21. *The Seventh Book of Revelations,* 7.31.2- 3, in Harris ed., *Birgitta of Sweden,* pp. 217-218. This quote is also recorded in *Life of Blessed Birgitta,* . 95, in ibid., p. 98.

22. Adam Easton, *Defensorium St. Birgittae,* trans. in James A. Schmidtke, "'Saving' by Faint Praise: St. Birgitta of Sweden, Adam Easton and Medieval Antifeminism, " *American Benedictine Review* 32, no.2 (June 1982), 160. See also *Extrauagancium,* 45:1-3, in Hollman, ed., *Heliga Birgittas,* p. 161.

23. Ibid.

24. Adam Easton, *Defensorium St. Birgittae,* trans. in James A. Schmidtke, "Adam Easton's Defense of St. Birgitta from Bodleian ms. Hamilton 7 Oxford University," Ph.D. diss. Duke University, 1971, art. 3.1.b and art. 3.2.b.

25. *Regula Salvatoris,* 12:153, in Eklund, ed., *Opera Minora,* p. 118.

26. Ibid., 14:167-170, pp. 120-121.

27. Ibid., 14:167, p. 120.

28. Adam Easton, *Defensorium,* in Schmidtke, "Adam Easton's Defense, " art. 7: l.c.

29. Ibid., art. 10:2.

30. *Solet annuere,* in *Constitution of Saint Coletta,* p. 102.

Chapter 7:
The Reformation Era

1. Joan Kelly Gadol, "Did Women Have a Renaissance?" in *Becoming Visible,* ed. R. Bridenthal, C. Koonz, and S. Stuard, 2nd ed. (Boston: Houghton Mifflin Co., 1987), pp. 176-201.

2. Carolyn Walker Bynum, *Holy Feast and Holy Fast* (Berkeley: University of California Press, 1987).

3. Marilyn Oliva, "Aristocracy or Meritocracy? Office Holding Patterns in Late Medieval English Nunneries." *Studies in Church History* 27 (1990), 197-208.

4. *AASS,* Mar. 9, 2:93-178, trans. in Georgian Fullerton, *St. Francis of Rome* (London: Catholic Truth Society, 1855), p. 101.

5. Ibid., p. 102.

6. Pierre Helyot, *Histoire des Ordres monastiques, religieux et militaires et des congregations seculieres* (Paris: Nicolas Gosselin, 1714), 7:303.

7. *The Rule of St. Angela Merici,* 18, trans. in M. Monica, *Angela Merici and Her Teaching Idea 1474-1540* (New York: Longman, Green and Company, 1927), p. 262.

8. Ibid., 1, p. 248.

9. Ibid., 2, p. 248.

10. Ibid., 18, p. 263.

11. Ibid., 19, p. 266.

12. Pius III, Ursuline Bull of Approbation, 1544, trans. in Monica, *Angela,* p. 322.

13. Session 25, ch. V, in *Canons and Decrees of the Council of Trent,* trans. H. J. Schroeder, 2nd ed. (Rockford, IL: Tan Books and Publishers, 1978), pp. 220-221.

14. Nicolas Onstenk, "De constitutione s. Pii V 'Circa Pastoralis' super clausura monialium and tertiarium, " *Periodica de re morali canonica liturgica* 39 (1950), 224-228.

15. As mentioned before, many papal pronouncements were simply not enforced. Cf. Carla Russo, *I monesteri femmineli di clausura a Napoli nel secolo XVII* (Naples: Università, 1970), to see what little effect the Tridentine edicts had on women's religious houses in Naples.

16. María Vela y Cuento, *Autobiografía y Libro de las Mercedes*, ed. and intro. O. González Hernández (Barcelona: Juan Flors, 1961), p. 335.

17. *The Life of Saint Teresa of Ávila by Herself*, trans. J. M. Cohen (London: Penguin Books, 1957), pp. 30-31.

18. Ibid., p. 51.

19. Ibid., p. 236.

20. Ibid., p. 237.

21. Ibid., pp. 270-271.

22. Ibid., p. 274.

23. Ibid., p. 275.

24. Teresa of Jesus, *Way of Perfection*, ch. 18, in *The Complete Works of Saint Teresa of Jesus*, trans. and ed. by E. Allison Peers (London: Sheed and Ward, 1975), 2:74.

25. Teresa of Jesus, *Spiritual Relations*, 19, in ibid., 1:344.

26. Teresa of Jesus, *Way of Perfection*, ch. 3, in ibid., 2:13.

Chapter 8:
The Transition into the Modern Age

1. Ana de San Bartolome, *Autobiografià*, 141, I, 348-349, para. 20, trans. A. Powell, in Electra Arenal and Stacey Schau, *Untold Sisters. Hispanic Nuns in Their Own Works* (Albuquerque: University of New Mexico Press, 1989), p. 64.

2. Alix Le Clerc, *Relation a la gloire de Dieu et de sa sainte Mère, et au salut de mon ame* (Nancy,1666), repr. in Alfred de Besancenet, *Le Bienheureux Pierre Fournier et la Lorraine* (Paris: René Muffat, Libraire, 1864), pp. 44-45.

3. *Autobiografià*, 143, in Arenal and Schau, *Sisters*, p. 64.

4. Ana de San Bartolome, *Letters*, 670-671, in ibid., p. 77.

5. Jean J. Surin, *Guide spiritual pour la perfection*, ed. M. de Certeau (Paris: Descleé De Brouwer, 1963), p. 101.

6. Pierre Fourier, *Sa Correspondence 1598-1640*, ed. Hélène Derréal and Madelline Cord'homme (Nancy: Pressus Universitaires de Nancy, 1987), 2:330.

7. Letter of July 22, 1619, in *Frances de Sales, Jane de Chantal: Letters of Spiritual Direction*, trans. P. M. Thibert (New York: Paulist Press, 1988), p. 239.

8. Francis de Sales, *Oeuvres de Saint Francois de Sales, Évêque de Genève et Docteur de l'Eglise Édition Complète*, ed. the Religious of the First Visitation Monastery of Annecy (Annecy: J. Niérat et al, 1892-1932), 25:338.

9. Preface to the Constitutions of the Visitation (1619), in ibid., 25:51.

10. Ibid., 25:223.

11. Ibid., 25:338.
12. Ibid., 17:406.
13. See Judith Combes Taylor, "From Proselytizing to Social Reform: Three Generations of French Female Teaching Congregations 1600-1720," Ph.D. diss. Arizona State University, 1980, app. 1, pp. 679-693. These Congregations are the Daughters of St. Agnes of Cambrai, Daughters of St. Agnes of Arras, Daughters of Charity, Sisters of St. Charles of Puy, Daughters of the Cross, Daughters of the Holy Spirit, Pious Daughters of Dammartin, Ladies of the Faith, Daughters of St. Genevieve, the Garden of Olive, Hospitallers of St. Joseph, Daughters of St. Joseph (Providence), Daughters of St. Martha, Sisters of Our Lady of Misericorde, New Catholics, Daughters of the Presentation, Daughters of the Providence of God, and Religious of the Incarnate Word and of the Holy Sacrament.
14. Letter 3B to Monsieur Vincent, May 1630, in *Spiritual Writings of Louise de Marillac. Correspondence and Thoughts*, ed. and trans. S. Louise Sullivan (Brooklyn: New City Press, 1991), p. 8.
15. Letter 6 to Monsieur Vincent, Dec. 1636, in ibid., p. 13.
16. *Order of the Day*, in ibid., pp. 726-727.
17. Draft of the Rule, in ibid., p. 727.
18. At least an additional fifty-six new communities were founded in France before the end of the century. Cf. Taylor, "Teaching Congregations," app. 3. No other country comes close to that quantity.
19. *Mémoires pour servir à l'histoire de Port-Royal, et à la Révérende Mère Marie-Angelique* (Utrecht, 1742), 1:262ff, in *The Nuns of Port-Royal as seen in their own narratives*, trans. M. E. Lowdes (London: Oxford University Press, 1909), p. 59.
20. Ibid., p. 63.
21. Ibid.
22. Ibid., p. 61.
23. *Letter to Nuncio Albergati*, in Mary C. E. Chambers, *The Life of Mary Ward 1585-1645*, ed. Henry James Coleridge (London: Burns and Oates, 1882-1885), 1:277-278.
24. Ibid., 1:283.
25. Ibid., 1:290.
26. Petition to Urban III, in ibid., 2:382.
27. María de San José, *Libro de recreaciones*, in Arenal and Schau, *Sisters*, p. 82; trans. p. 95.
28. "Three Speeches of our Reverend Mother Chief Superior made at St. Omer, having been long absent," trans. in Chambers, *Mary Ward*, 1:408.
29. Ibid., 1:410.
30. Ibid., 1:413-414.
31. Ibid. 1:410.

Selected Secondary Sources

Chapter 1: The Beginning

Clark, Elizabeth A. "Ascetic Renunciation and Feminine Advancement: A Paradox of Late Ancient Christianity." *Anglican Theological Review* 63 (July 1981), 240-257.

———."Authority and Humility: A Conflict of Values in Fourth-Century Female Monasticism." *Byzantinische Forschungen* 9 (1985), 17-33.

Clarke, W. K. Lowther. *St. Basil the Great. A Study in Monasticism*. Cambridge: Cambridge University Press, 1913.

Duchesne, L. "La vie des père du Jura." *Melanges d'archeologie et d'histoire* 18 (1893), 3-16.

Elm, Susanne. "Evagrius Ponticus' *Sententiae ad Virginem*." *Dumbarton Oaks Papers* 45 (1991), 97-120.

Jerome. *The Pilgrimage of the Holy Paula*. Translated by Aubrey Stewart. London: Palestine Pilgrims Text Society, 1887.

King, Margot H. *The Desert Mothers. A Bibliography*. Saskatoon: Peregrina Publishing Co., 1984.

LaPorte, Jean. *The Role of Women in Early Christianity*. New York: The Edwin Mellon Press, 1982.

Malady, Tadros Y. "Early Monasticism Among Women in the Coptic Church." *Studia Patristica* 19 (1989), 111-116.

Murphy, Francis X. "Melanie the Elder: A Bibliographical Note." *Traditio* 5 (1947), 59-77.

———. *Rufinus of Aquileia (345-411). His Life and Works*. Washington, D.C.: The Catholic University of America Press, 1945.

Rader, Rosemary. "Early Christian Forms of Communal Spirituality: Women's Communities." In *The Continuing Quest for God*, ed. William Skudlarek, pp. 88-99. Collegeville, MN: The Liturgical Press, 1982.

Simpson, Jane. "Women and Asceticism in the Fourth-Century: A Question of Interpretation." *Journal of Religious History* 15, no. 2 (June 1988), 38-60.

Topping, Eva. "Thekla the Nun: In Praise of Women." *Greek Orthodox Theological Review* 25 (Winter, 1980), 353-370.

Ward, Benedicta. "Apophthegmata Matrum." *Studia Patristica* 16, no. 2 (1985), 63-66.

White, Joan. "The Development and Eclipse of the Deacon-abbess." *Studia Patristica* 19 (1989), 111-116.

Yarbrough, Anne. "Christianization in the Fourth-Century: The Example of Roman Women." *Church History* 45 (June 1976), 149-165.

Chapter 2: Women Religious in the Early Medieval West

Andre, J. "Widows and vowesses." *The Archaeological Journal* 49 (1892), 69-82.

Bateson, Mary. "Origin and Early History of Double Monasteries." *Transactions of the Royal Historical Society* 13 n.s. (1899), 137-198.

Bellenger, Aidan. "Chariots of Aminadab. English Double Monasteries." *Word and Spirit* 11 (1989), 41-49.

Bitel, Lisa M. "Women's Monastic Enclosures in Early Ireland: A Study of Female Spirituality and Male Monastic Mentalities." *Journal of Medieval History* 12 (1986), 15-36.

Byrne, Mary. *The Tradition of the Nun in Medieval England.* Washington, D.C.: The Catholic University of America Press, 1932.

Emmanuel, M. "Saint Walburga." *Word and Spirit* 11 (1989), 50-59.

Esposito, Mario. "On the Earliest Latin Life of St. Brigid of Kildare." *Proceedings of the Royal Irish Academy* 30 (1912), 307-326.

Godfrey, John. "The Double Monastery in Early English History." *The Ampleforth Journal* 79 (1974), 19-32.

Hochstetler, Donald. "The Meaning of Monastic Cloister for Women According to Caesarius of Arles." In *Religion, Culture and Society in Early Middle Ages,* ed. Thomas F. X. Noble and John J. Contreni, pp. 27-40. Kalamazoo, MI: Medieval Institute Publications, 1987.

Lanigan, John. *An Ecclesiastical History of Ireland . . . from Irish Annals and Other Authentic Documents, Still Existing in Manuscripts,* 2nd ed. Dublin: J. Cumming, 1829.

Mayo, Hope. "The Sources of Female Monasticism in Merovingian Gaul." *Studia Patristica* 16, no. 2 (1985), 32-37.

McNamara, JoAnn. "The Ordeal of Community: Hagiography and Discipline in Merovingian Convents." *Vox Benedicta* 3 (October 1986), 293-326.

———. "The Rule of Donatus of Besançon. A Working Translation." *Vox Benedicta* 2, no. 2 (April 1985), 85-107; 2, no. 3 (July 1985), 181-204.

Olphe-Galliard, M. "Consecrated Virginity in the Latin West." In *Chastity,* trans. L. C. Sheppard, pp. 57-76. Westminster, MD: The Newman Press, 1963.

Reynolds, Roger. "*Virgines subintroductae* in Celtic Christianity." *Harvard Theological Review* 61 (1968), 547-566.

Thompson, A. Hamilton. "Double Monasteries and the Male Element in Nunneries." In *The Ministry of Women.* Edited by a committee appointed by the Archbishop of Canterbury, pp. 145-164. London: Society for Promoting Christian Knowledge, 1919.

Vogüe, Adalbert de. "Caesarius of Arles and the Origin of the Enclosure of Nuns." *Word and Spirit* 11 (1989), 16-29.

Wemple, Suzanne F. "Contemplative Life: The Search for Feminine Autonomy in the Frankish Kingdom." *Anima* 6, no. 2 (Spring,1980), 131-136.

———. *Women in Frankish Society.* Philadelphia: University of Pennsylvania Press, 1981.

Chapter 3: Restriction and Revival

Bateson, Mary. "Rules for Monks and Canons after the Revival under King Edgar." *English Historical Review* 9 (1894), 690-708.

Bonfante, Larissa. *The Plays of Hrotswitha of Gandersheim.* New York: New York University Press, 1979.

Edwards, Eanswythe. "St. Eanswythe of Folkestone." *Word and Spirit* 11 (1989), 30-40.

Goscelin of Canterbury. "La vie de Sainte Vulfhilde." *Analecta Bollandiana* 32 (1913), 10-26.

Hamilton, Bernard. "The Monastic Revival in Tenth Century Rome." *Studia Monastica* 4 (1962), 35-68.

Heinrich, Mary P. *The Canonesses and Education in the Early Middle Ages.* Washington, D.C.: The Catholic University of America Press, 1924.

Hilpisch, Stephanus. *History of Benedictine Nuns.* Translated by M. Joanne Muggli. Collegeville, MN: St. John's Abbey Press, 1958.

Hudson, William H. "Hrotsvitha of Gandersheim." *English Historical Review* 3 (1888), 431-457.

The Nun's Rule being the Ancren Riewle modernized by James Morton with introduction by Abbot Gasquet. London: Chatto and Windus, 1926.

Power, Eileen. *Medieval English Nunneries.* Reprint. New York: Biblio and Tanner, 1964.

Savage, Anne, and Nicholas Watson, trans. *Anchoritic Spirituality. "Ancrene Wisse" and Associated Works.* New York: Paulist Press, 1991.

Schulenburg, Jane Tibbetts. "Strict Active Enclosure and Its Effect on the Female Monastic Experience (ca. 500-1100)." In *Medieval Religious Women*, vol. 1: *Distant Echoes*, ed. John A. Nichols and Lillian Shank, pp. 51-86. Kalamazoo, MI: Cistercian Publications, 1984.

Steele, Francesca M. *Anchoresses of the West.* London: Sands and Co., 1903.

Verdon, Jean. "Notes sur le rôle économique des monastères féminins en France dans la seconde moitié du IXe-et au début du Xe siècle." *Revue Mabillon* 58 (1975), 329-343.

———. "Recherches sur les monastères féminins dans la France du sud aux IXe-XIe siècles." *Annales du Midi* 88 (1976), 117-138.

Warren, Ann K. *Anchorites and Their Patrons in Medieval England.* Berkeley: University of California Press, 1985.

Chapter 4: The Fruits of the Monastic Revival

Becquet, J. "Les institutions de l'Ordre de Grandmont au Moyen-Age." *Revue Mabillon* 42 (1952), 31-42.

———. "Les premiers écrivains de l'Ordre de Grandmont." *Revue Mabillon* 42 (1953), 21-37.

Boyd, Catherine E. *A Cistercian Nunnery in Medieval Italy.* Cambridge, MA: Harvard University Press, 1943.

Clark, Anne L. *Elizabeth of Shönau.* Philadelphia: University of Pennsyvania Press, 1992.

Colvin, H. M. *The White Canons in England.* Oxford: Clarendon Press, 1951.

Constable, Giles. "Aelred of Rievaulx and the Nun of Watton: An Episode in the Early History of the Gilbertine Order." *Studies in Church History,* subs. 1 (1978), 205-226.

Crens, A. "Les Soeurs dan l'ordre de Prémontré." *Analecta Praemonstratensia* 5 (1929), 5-26.

Dalarun, Jacques. "Le véritable fin de Robert d'Arbrissel (d'après une pièce inconnue du dossier hagiographique)." *Cahiers de Civilisation Medievale* 27 (October-December 1984), 303-317.

Dimier, M. "Chapitres generaux d'abbesses cisterciennes." *Cîteaux* 11 (1960), 268-273.

Fontette, Micheline de. *Les religieuses a l'age du droit canon. Recherches sur les structures juridiques des branches féminines des ordres.* Paris: Librairie Philosophique J. Vrin, 1967.

Elm, Kasper, ed. *Norbert von Xanten.* Cologne: Weinard, 1984.

Forey, A. J. "Women and the Military Orders in the 12th and 13th Century." *Studia Monastica* 29 (1987), 63-92.

Gaussin, Pierre-Roger. "Les communautés féminines dans l'espace Languedocien de la fin du XIe à la fin du XIVe s." In *La Femme dans la vie religieuse du Languedoc (XIIIe-XIVe s),* ed. M. H. Vicaire, 299-332. Toulouse: Fanjeaux, 1988.

Gold, Penny S. *The Lady and the Virgin.* Chicago: University of Chicago Press, 1985.

Graham, Rose. *S. Gilbert of Sempringham and the Gilbertines.* London: Elliot Stock, 1901.

Hunt, Noreen. "Notes on the History of Benedictine and Cistercian Nuns in Britain." *Cistercian Studies* 8 (1973), 157-177.

Kelso, Carl Jr. "Women and Power: Fontevrault and the Paraclete Compared." *Comitatus* 22 (1991), 55-69.

Lopez, Amancio R. *El Real Monasterio de las Huelgas de Burgos y Hospital del Rey.* Burgos: Centro Católico, 1907.

Milis, Ludo. *L'ordre des chanoines reguliers d'Arrouaise.* Brugge: De Tempel, 1969.

Nichols, John A. "The Internal Organization of English Cistercian Nunneries." *Cîteaux, commentarii cistercienses* 30 (1979), 23-40.

Smith, Jacqueline. "Robert of Arbrissel: *Procurator Mulierum.*" *Studies in Church History,* subs.1 (1978), 175-184.

Thompson, Sally. *Women Religious.* Oxford: Clarendon Press, 1991.

Verdon, Jean. "Les sources de l'histoire de la femme en Occident aux Xe-XIIIe siècles." *Cahiers de Civilisation Medievale* 19 (1976), 247-264.

Williams, David H. "Cistercian Nunneries in Medieval Wales." *Cîteaux, commentarii cistercienses* 26 (1975), 155-174.

Chapter 5: The Appeal of the *Vita Apostolica*

Brooke, R. B. and C. N. L. "St Clare." *Studies in Church History,* subs. 1 (1978), 257-287.

Bynum, Carolyn Walker. "Women Mystics in the Thirteenth-Century: The Cases of the Nuns of Helta. "In *Jesus as Mother*, ed. Carolyn Walker Bynum, pp. 170-262. Berkeley: University of California Press, 1982.

Cawley, Martinus. "Our Lady and the Nuns and Monks of XIII-Century Belguim." *Word and Spirit* 10 (1988), 94-128.

Delmaire, Bernard. "Les béguines dans le Nord de la France au premièr siècle de leur histoire (vers 1230-vers 1350)." In *Les religieuses en France au XIIIe siècle*, ed. Michel Parisse, 121-162. Nancy: Presses Universitaires, 1985.

Gazeau, Roger. "La cloture des moniales au XIIe siècle en France." *Revue Mabillon* 58 (1974), 289-308.

Gertrude of Helfta. *Les exercices. Oeuvres Spirituelles*. Paris: Sources Chrétiennes, 1967.

Grau, E. "Das Privilegium paupertatis der hl. Klara. Geschichte und Beteutung." *Wissenchaft und Weisheit* 38 (1975), 17-25.

Greven, Joseph. "Der Ursprung des Beginenwesens." *Historisches Jahrbuch* 35 (1914), 26-58.

Grundmann, Herbert. *Religiöse Bewegungen im Mittelalter*. Berlin: E. Ebering, 1935.

Hadejewijch. The Complete Works. Translated by M. Columba Hart. New York: Paulist Press, 1980.

Jordan of Saxony. *Love Among the Saints. The Letters of Bl. Jordan of Saxony to Bl. Diana of Andalo*. Translated by Kathleeen Pond. London: Bloomsbury Publishing Co., 1958.

———. *The New Life of St. Dominic*. Translated by E. McEniry. Columbus, OH: The Columban Press, 1926.

Lambert, Malcolm. *Medieval Heresy*, 2nd ed. Oxford: Blackwell, 1992.

Lazzeri, Z. "Il 'privilegium paupertatis' concesso da Innocenzo III e che cose fossa inorogone." *Archivum franciscanum historicum* 11 (1918), 270-276.

Little, A. G. *A Guide to Franciscan Studies*. London: SPCK, 1920.

McDonnell, Ernest. *The Beguines and Beghards in Medieval Culture*. New Brunswick, NJ: Rutgers University Press, 1954.

Mechthild of Hackeborn. *The Book of Costlye Grace of Mechthild of Hackeborn*. Edited by Theresa Halligan. Toronto: Pontifical Institute of Medieval Studies, 1979.

Mechthild of Madgeburg. *Das Fliessende Licht der Gottheit*. Translated by M. Schmidt. Zurich: Einsiedeln, 1955.

Moore, R. I. *The Origins of European Dissent*. London: Allen Lane, 1977.

Oliger, P. L. "De Origine Regularum Ordinis S. Clarae." *Archivum franciscanum historicum* 5 (1912), 181-209; 413-447.

Phillips, Dayton. "Beguines in Medieval Strasburg. A Study of the Social Aspect of Beguine Life." Ph.D. diss., Stanford University, 1941.

Ranft, Patricia. "An Overturned Victory: Clare of Assisi and the Thirteenth-Century Church." *Journal of Medieval History* 17 (1991), 123-134.

Robeck, Nesta de. *St Clare of Assisi*. Milwaukee: Bruce Publishing Co., 1951.

Sabatier, Paul. "Le privilège de la pauvreté." *Revue historie franciscaine* 1 (1924), 1-54.

Simon, Andre. *L'ordre des Pénitentes de Sts. Marie-Madeleine en Allemagne au XIIIme Siècle*. Fribourg: Librairie de l'Oeuvre de Saint-Paul, 1918.

Simon, W. "The Beguine Movement in the Southern Low Countries: A Reassessment." *Bulletin de l'Institut historique belge de Rome* 59 (1989), 63-105.

Wadding, Luc, and J. M. Forseca, eds. *Annales minorum seu trium ordinum*, 3rd ed. Quaracchi: Ad Claras Aquas, 1831.

Chapter 6: The Visionary Late Medieval Period

Alencon, Ubald d'. *Documents sur la Réforme de sainte Colette en France.* Paris: Picard, 1908.

Bolton, Brenda. "Innocent III's Treatment of the Humiliati." *Studies in Church History* 8 (1972), 73-82.

———. "Sources for the Early History of the Humiliati." *Studies in Church History* 11 (1975), 125-133.

Cnattingius, Hans. *Studies on the Order of St. Bridget of Sweden.* Stockholm: Almqvist and Wiksell, 1963.

Colledge, E. "Epistola solitarii ad regis." *Medieval Studies* 17 (1956), 19-49.

Daichman, Graciela S. "Misconduct in the Medieval Nunnery: Fact, not Fiction." In *That Gentle Strength,* ed. L. Coon, K. Haldone, and E. Sommer, pp. 97-117. Charlottesville: University Press of Virginia, 1992.

Gill, Katherine. "Open Monasteries for Women in Late Medieval and Early Modern Italy: Two Roman Examples." In *The Crannied Wall,* ed. Craig A. Monson, pp. 15-47. Ann Arbor: University of Michigan Press, 1992.

Hyma, Albert. *The Brethren of the Common Life.* Grand Rapids, MI: Wm. B. Eerdmans Publishing Company, 1950.

———. *The Christian Renaissance.* Grand Rapids, MI: Wm. B. Eerdmans Publishing Company, 1950.

Jørgensen, Johannes. *Saint Bridget of Sweden.* Translated by I. Lund. 2 vols. London: Longmans, 1954.

Lagorio, Valerie. "The Medieval Continental Women Mystics: An Introduction." In *An Introduction to the Medieval Mystics of Europe,* ed. Paul E. Szarmach, pp. 161-193. Albany: State University of New York Press, 1984.

Leon, P. *Lives of the Saints and Blessed of the Three Orders of St. Francis, translated from Aureole Seraphique of the Very Rev. Father Leon.* Tauton, MA: Franciscan Convent, 1866.

Knowles, David, and R.N. Hadcock. *Medieval Religious Houses: England and Wales.* New York: St. Martin's Press, 1971.

Post, R. R. *The Modern Devotion.* Leiden: E. J. Brill, 1968.

Scott, Karen. "'Io Catarina': Ecclesiastical Politics and Oral Culture in the Letters of Catherine of Siena." In *Dear Sister. Medieval Women and the Epistolary Genre,* ed. Karen Cherewatuk and Ulrike Wiethaus, pp. 87-121. Philadelphia: University of Pennsylvania Press, 1993.

Weiler, A. G. "Recent Historiography on the Modern Devotion: Some Debated Questions." *Archief voor de geschiedenis van de Katholieke Kerk in Nederland* 27 (1985), 161-175.

Chapter 7: The Reformation Era

Anson, Peter. "Papal Enclosure for Nuns." *Cistercian Studies* 3 (1968), 109-123.

Cain, James R. "Cloister and the Apostolate of Religious Women." *Review for Religious* 27 (1968), 243-280; 427-448; 653-671; 916-937.

Cocheril, Maur. "Les abbesses de Lorvaõ au XVIe siècle." *Revue d'historie ecclésiastique* 55 (1960), 916-935.

Cohen, Sherrill. "Asylums for Women in Counter-Reformation Italy." In *Women in Reformation and Counter Reformation Europe*, ed. Sherrin Marshall, pp. 166-188. Bloomington: University of Indiana Press, 1989.

Kavanaugh, Kieran. "St. Teresa and the Spirituality of Sixteenth-Century Spain." In *The Roots of the Modern Christian Tradition*, ed. E. Rozanne Elder, pp. 91-104. Kalamazoo, MI: Cistercian Publications, 1984.

Lemaitre, Henri. "Le Couvent des Soeurs Grises à Comines." *La France franciscaine* 2 (1913), 277-313.

———. "Les Soins Hospitaliers a domicile donnés dès le XIVe siècle." *Revue d'historie franciscaine* 1 (1924), 180-208.

———. "Statuts des Religieuses du Tiers Ordre Franciscain dites Soeurs Grises Hospitalieres (1483)." *Archivum franciscanum historicum* 4 (1911), 713-731.

Lowe, K. J. "Female Strategies for Success in a Male-Ordered World: The Benedictine Convent of Le Murate in Florence in the Fifteenth and Early Sixteenth Centuries." In *Studies in Church History* 27 (1990), 209-221.

María de Santo Domingo. *Libro de la Oración de Sor María de Santo Domingo.* Introduction by Jose M. Blecua. Madrid: Hauser y Menet, 1948.

María Vela. *The Third Mystic of Ávila: The Self-Revelation of María Vela, a 16th Century Nun.* Translated by Frances P. Keyes. New York: Straus and Cudahy, 1960.

McLaughlin, Mary M. "Creating and Recreating Communities of Women: The Case of Corpus Domini, Ferrara, 1406-1452." In *Sisters and Workers in the Middle Ages*, ed. Judith M. Bennett et al., pp. 261-288. Chicago: University of Chicago Press, 1989.

O'Dwyer, Peter. "The Carmelite Order in Pre-Reformation Ireland." *Irish Ecclesiastical Record* 110 (December 1968), 350-363.

Perry, Mary E. "Beatas and the Inquisition in Early Modern Seville." In *Inquisition and Society in Early Modern Europe*, ed. Stephen Haliczer, pp. 147-168. Totowa, NJ: Barnes and Noble, 1987.

Pond, Kathleen, trans. *The Spirit of Spanish Mystics. An Anthology of Spanish Religious Prose from the 15th to 17th Century.* New York: P. J. Kenedy and Sons, 1958.

Ramge, Sebastian. *An Introduction to the Writings of Saint Teresa.* Chicago: Henry Regnery Co., 1963.

Ranft, Patricia. "A Key to Counter Reformation Women's Activism: The Confessor-Spiritual Director." *Journal of Feminist Studies in Religion* 10, no. 2 (Fall 1994), 7-26.

Rivet, Mary M. *The Influence of the Spanish Mystics on the Works of Saint Francis de Sales.* Washington, D.C.: The Catholic University of Amercia Press, 1941.

Shields, Maria. "St. Teresa and Eastern Christian Monastic Tradition." *Spiritual Life* 23 (Fall 1977), 153-162.

Valone, Carolyn. "Roman Matrons as Patrons: Various Views of the Cloister Wall." In *The Crannied Wall*, ed. Craig A. Monson, pp. 49-72. Ann Arbor: University of Michigan Press, 1992.

Chapter 8: The Transition into the Modern Age

Biver, Paul, and Marie. *Abbayes, monastéres, couvents de femmes a Paris des origines a la fin du XVIIIe siècle.* Paris: Presses Universitaire de France, 1975.

Bremond, Henri. *A Literary History of Religious Thought in France.* Translated by K. L. Montgomery. London: SPCK, 1936.

Dagens, Jean. *Bérulle et les Origines de la Restauration catholique (1575-1611).* Paris: Descleé de Brouwer, 1952.

Ériau, J. B. *La Vénérable Madeleine de St.Joseph.* Paris: L'Art Catholique, 1921.

Forster, Ann M. C. "The Chronicles of the English Poor Clares of Rouen-I." *Recusant History* 18 (May 1986), 59-102.

Gazier, Augustin. *Jeanne de Chantal et Angelique Arnauld d'après leur correspondance (1620-1641). Étude Historique et Critique.* Westminster, MD: The Newman Press, 1963.

Guesdre, M.-C. "Le femme et la vie spirituelle." *XVIIe Siécle* 62-63 (1964), 47-77.

Guilday, Peter. *The English Catholic Refugees on the Continent.* London: Longmans, 1914.

Hervé-Bazin, F. *Les Grands Ordres et Congregations de Femme.* Paris: Libraire Victor Lecoffre, 1889.

Hicks, Leo. "Mary Ward's Great Enterprise." *The Month* 151 (1928), 137-146; 152 (1928), 40-52; 231-238; 153 (1929), 40-48; 223-236.

Marmion, John P. "Some Notes of the 'Painted Life' of Mary Ward." *Recusant History* 18, no. 3 (May 1987), 318-322.

Menthon, Alexandre de. *Les Deux Filles de Sainte Chantal.* Annecy: Monastère de la Visitation, 1913.

Sedgwich, Alexander. *Jansenism in Seventeenth-Century France.* Charlottesville: University Press of Virginia, 1977.

Stopp, Elizabeth. *Madame de Chantal.* Westminster, MD: The Newman Press, 1963.

Thompson, William M, ed. *Bérulle and the French School: Selected Writings.* Translated by Lowell M. Glendon. New York: Paulist Press, 1989.

Weaver, F. "Erudition, Spirituality, and Women: The Jansenist Contribution." In *Women in Reformation and Counter Reformation Europe*, ed. Sherrin Marshall, pp.189-207. Bloomington: University of Indiana Press,1989.

———. *The Evolution of the Reform of Port-Royal.* Paris: Beauchesne, 1978.

Wright, Wendy M. *Bond of Perfection.* New York: Paulist Press, 1985.

———. "Two Faces of Christ: Jeanne de Chantal." In *Peaceweavers,* vol. 2, *Medieval Religious Women,* ed. John A. Nichols and Lillian T. Shank, pp. 335-364. Kalamazoo, MI: Cistercian Publications, 1987.

Williams, Charles E. *The French Oratorians and Absolutism, 1611-1641.* New York: Peter Lang, 1989.

Index